Why
CATHOLICS
DON'T GIVE
...And What Can Be Done About It

CHARLES E. ZECH

Introduction by
FRANCIS J. BUTLER

Our Sunday Visitor Publishing Division
Our Sunday Visitor, Inc.
Huntington, Indiana 46750

Copyright © 2000 by Our Sunday Visitor Publishing Division, Our Sunday Visitor, Inc.

International Standard Book Number: 0-87973-706-9
Library of Congress Catalog Card Number: 99-75033

Cover design by Rebecca Heaston

Printed in the United States of America

Contents

Acknowledgements

This study could not have been possible without a great deal of support, assistance, and advice. Major funding came from the Lilly Endowment, Inc., a private foundation interested in the study of religion. They generously supported this work with two separate grants. The first underwrote my participation in The American Congregational Giving Study, and the second allowed me to focus just on the data for Catholics in our sample and write this book. While the entire Lilly staff has been a delight to work with, I'm especially grateful for the encouragement and support offered by Fred Hofheinz, Program Officer in Religion at Lilly.

Many of my views on religious giving were sharpened while I was a participant in the Project on Non-Profit Organizations at Yale University, another Lilly-funded project. All of the members of that seminar contributed to the development of my understanding of religious giving, but I am especially grateful for the insights gained from discussions with Scott Cormode, Jim Davidson, Thom Jeavons, Greg Krohn, and David Roozen.

Pete Zaleski, my colleague and frequent co-author from Villanova's Economics Department, has been patient and generous with his time in answering my questions about various statistical methodologies. Dave Reid, a stewardship and development professional, read a draft of the manuscript and offered valuable advice from his unique perspective.

My undergraduate research assistant, John Cacchione, and my graduate assistants, Ricardo Martinez and Dennis McCafferty, were all wonderfully understanding in meeting short deadlines, and consistently provided me with superior quality work.

This study relied on the data collected from the Lilly-funded American Congregational Giving Study. I am grateful to the bishops in the nine U.S. dioceses where data collection took place for their cooperation; to the 125 parish pastors who completed the parish profile surveys and enabled us to survey their parishioners; and to the nearly 2,200 Catholic laypersons who returned completed surveys. This was an enormous project, and was truly a team effort among Dean Hoge, Patrick McNamara, Michael Donahue, and myself. Together we developed and tested the survey materials. We spent many hours convening in person and in conference calls, bouncing ideas off one another. Each of us was responsible for the actual data collection in various parts of the country. Our many discussions were instrumental in helping to frame my interpretation of the data. For all of these reasons, even though I am responsible for the writing of this book and the interpretations that appear in it, the book is written using the comradely "we" in recognition of their contribution. But for heaven's sake, don't blame them for any errors or misinterpretations that appear.

My wife, Ann, herself an economist and graduate theology student, served as a sounding board and filter for my analysis, and offered me the type of encouragement that no one else could. My children, Tom, Trish, John, and Ron, graciously gave up time with their dad, and (sometimes begrudgingly) occasionally took over my share of the household chores while I worked on this book.

To the extent that this book is part of my own faith journey, I acknowledge a special debt of gratitude to my small faith community: Ann, Bob, Rosemary, Glenn, Marian, Tim, Kathleen, Anna, Lois, Bill, Ellie, and Margaret. They have been a constant source of inspiration, always moving me in the right direction, both through their example and their wisdom. They represent the best of everything that the Catholic Church has to offer. It is to them that this book is dedicated.

Charles Zech
Villanova, Pennsylvania
March 1999

Foreword

When it comes to charitable giving and Catholics, few would argue with the Dickensian aphorism that it is both the worst and best of times. Archdioceses and dioceses are reporting a resurgence of interest and donations for Catholic schools, the formation of newly endowed foundations, deferred-giving programs, and other signs of new resources. At the same time, most Catholic parishes continue to finance themselves from the same narrow base of parishioner donors, some 75% of the money in a typical parish being given by 25% of the people.

For 11 years, starting with work from the Gallup organization and Independent Sector, research on the giving and volunteering habits of individuals identified by faith affiliation has been fueling a vigorous debate within Catholicism. Are Catholics really the woeful under-performing donors that many have claimed? Why do Catholics appear to give at half the rate of their Protestant counterparts? With increasing numbers of Catholics, 25% of the U.S. population, and their accelerating social and economic nobility, why aren't nationwide parish appeals of the hierarchy growing? Why are too many dioceses and parishes having to make such strenuous efforts simply to keep themselves afloat?

Within this setting of growing financial stringency, it has become clear to the nation's bishops that the Church lacked a spirituality that would help Catholics participate more deeply and supportively in the Church's ministries. Thus, the hierarchy published the pastoral letter "Stewardship: A Disciple's Response," a national call to Catholics to examine their consciences, not just on the issue of money, but on how people of faith used their time and their personal gifts in service to others and to the Church.

Though many major donors thought a more direct approach to the discussion of money and church finances was needed when the letter was issued in 1992, few disagree that the bishops gave Catholics a new language, vision, and set of questions with which to examine their priorities. The letter has set a new context for discussions on Catholic ministry and its resources in many dioceses and parishes across the land.

Still, eight years later, very few financial indicators show significant change in the giving habits of Catholics. Generally, Catholics continue not to pledge and give in a planned manner. They persistently decide weekly whether and how much to give. Annual household donations by Catholics are only one-third of the donations given by Assemblies of God members, one-half of the donations of Baptists and Presbyterians, and well below donations of Lutherans.

Thanks to the determination of scholars like Dr. Charles Zech, we are beginning to unlock the mysteries of Catholic giving. Through Dr. Zech's efforts, we can now see just how interwoven are the giving habits of Catholics and the quality of parish life. When Catholics have a voice in the financial decisions of their parishes and understand how donated funds are used, they behave differently as donors and volunteers. Conversely, where giving is low among Catholics, one can now confidently suspect that a poor connection to the Church and its work is being made. In short, readers of *Why Catholics Don't Give* will learn the salubrious difference that a theology of stewardship can make when it really permeates parish life.

For this, pastors, pastoral councils, Catholic school-boards, and diocesan and parish staff will find Dr. Zech's book hard to put down. Readers will discover a treasure trove of findings bearing on Catholic constituencies. Chapter by chapter, the book unfolds the fascinating story of how inclusion, accountability, and a spiritually grounded stewardship drive enthusiasm and support for the Church's mission.

The relevance of Dr. Zech's work extends far beyond capital campaigns, Lenten appeals, and other fund-raising programs. Its special importance can be seen in the light of the Church's work in the next century. It is then that a whole new generation of Catholics, who are growing up in an era marked by individualism and suspicion of institutions, will determine the level of Church resources for its mission. Dr. Zech has found that decision-making styles with which the Church operates makes a pronounced difference with this post-Vatican II generation. They will demand greater financial accountability and more say in how their parishes are run.

It is interesting to note that recent social research forecasts a return to religiosity in America in the next century. People will come to religion because of their desire for community in a world increasingly starved for a sense of connection to others. This presents a great evangelizing opportunity for the Catholic Church. But welcoming and reconciling outreach to spiritually searching Americans will only happen when parishioners are excited about belonging to the Church and share enthusiastically in its mission.

Wise pastors know this, and because they do, they will find *Why Catholics Don't Give* an invaluable guide as they seek to deepen the faith commitment and the financial covenant with their flock. Successful religious institutions in the next century will be those that set a course now to be good stewards striving to be accountable and thereby engaging their members as active participants in the Church's mission.

Dr. Francis J. Butler, President
Foundations and Donors Interested in Catholic Activities, Inc.

1

Introduction to Catholic Giving

Catholics contribute less money to their churches than do members of nearly every other major U.S. religion. This statement might have raised some eyebrows 20 years ago, but by now it has been firmly supported by mounds of evidence. Study after study has shown Catholics to be less generous to their churches, no matter how that generosity is measured (giving per member, giving per household, giving as a percent of income, etc.).

Just as one example, Figure 1-1 shows how Catholics stack up against other major U.S. religions in giving as a percent of income. The data was collected by Stephen Hart from the General Social Survey for the period 1987-1989. As might be expected, Catholics are well behind the more conservative, evangelical denominations, such as Mormons, who teach tithing as biblically mandated and therefore an integral part of their Christian duty. But Catholics also lag behind the more liberal, mainline Protestant Churches, like Methodists and Presbyterians, whose teachings on the Bible frequently do not differ much from their own. While this data is from the late 1980s, every indication is that this pattern still prevails today.

Father Andrew Greeley and Bishop William McManus (1987) were among the first to shed some light on this phenomenon. They looked at Catholic giving over a 25-year period, from 1960 to the mid-1980s, using data from six different surveys. They found an interesting trend. While in the early 1960s Catholics gave approximately the same percent of income to their church as did mainline Protestants (about 2.2% for both groups), by the late 1970s and through the 1980s Protestant giving as a percent of income had remained relatively constant at 2.2%, while Catholic giving had been cut in half to about 1.1%.

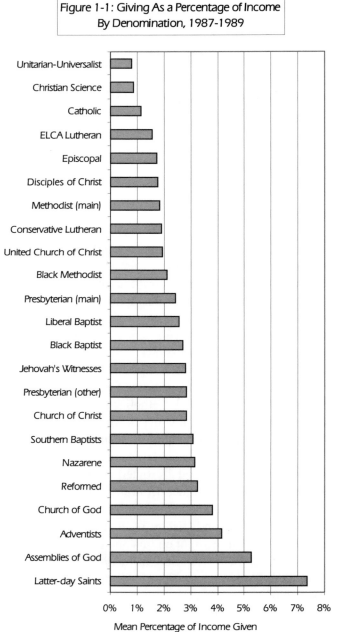

Figure 1-1: Giving As a Percentage of Income
By Denomination, 1987-1989

Mean Percentage of Income Given
Data is based on responses by persons who attend services at least yearly.
Data from General Social Survey, 1987-1989.

Subsequent researchers have found a similar pattern, consistently observing that Catholics give at about half the rate of Protestants, although the specific levels of giving differ from study to study. For example, the Independent Sector, a Washington-based coalition of organizations interested in philanthropy and voluntary action, commissioned a series of surveys conducted by the Gallup Organization to provide insights into charitable contributions of both time and money among Americans. While the actual figures differed slightly from year to year because of sampling variation, the pattern of Catholics giving at roughly half the rate of Protestants generally held. For example, figures for 1988 showed Catholics contributing 0.6% of their income to their church, while Protestants contributed 1.0%; the respective figures for 1990 were 1.3% and 2.4%. Dean Hoge and Fenggang Yang (1994) of Catholic University analyzed data from the 1987-89 General Social Surveys and found Catholics giving 1.2% of their income versus 2.4% for Protestants. Finally, using data from a 1987 survey of 201 congregations (54 Catholic, 147 Protestant) Peter Zaleski and Charles Zech (1994) found Catholic contributions to lag even further behind — $96 per capita versus $297 per person in the Protestant churches.

Unfortunately, since all of these studies use data collected from the mid-1980s or later, none of them have been able to confirm that Catholics at one time gave at the same rate as mainline Protestants and have since slipped, a trend that was so critical to Greeley's and McManus's analysis. But past trends aren't our main concern here. We are interested in the present and the future.

So What?

The low giving of Catholics is not merely of academic interest. It has important ramifications for the Church as it moves into the next millennium. The Church needs all the support it can get to carry out its mission.

Joseph Harris (1994) has estimated that low Catholic giving in the United States costs the Church $1.963 billion a year. That's how much more he estimates that the Church could collect annually if Catholics gave at the average rate for all Americans. Just think what the Church is missing because it doesn't have this $2 billion! Parishes and parish schools have been closed because of financial pressures, many in our inner cities where their presence is most urgent. Maintenance on buildings has been deferred, until it is too late to salvage some otherwise useful facilities. Parishes have been unable to meet the demands of equity as set forth in the U.S. bishops' own pastoral letter, "Economic Justice for All," in paying a fair wage to their staff and parochial schoolteachers. The Church faces huge, unfunded retirement costs for its priests and religious. And of course there is the ongoing work of supporting Catholic social-service agencies in this country, and funding missionaries trying to spread the faith around the world. Sometimes these ramifications have led to dramatic consequences. Joseph Harris (1994) cites the situation in the Chicago Archdiocese, where in 1993 the late Cardinal Bernardin stated, "We will be broke in four years if the Chicago Archdiocese does not address its financial problems immediately." At that point, annual archdiocesan deficits were running in the range of $12 to $15 million a year. Harris goes on to observe that the Chicago situation, while noteworthy because of the vast amounts of money involved, isn't all that unique. He pointed to a study in the *National Catholic Reporter* (Windsor, 1990) that estimated that 10-20% of all U.S. dioceses are operating with a budgetary deficit, while others have already had to make drastic cuts in critical ministries and services in an effort to prevent financial catastrophe.

Everybody Has a Theory

Why is Catholic giving so low? Why do Catholics contribute so much less to their church than their neighbors who belong to other Christian churches? Are Catholics cheap? Are they less religious? Are they ignorant?

Most researchers who have studied the low level of Catholic giving have felt obliged to offer an explanation. When Father Andrew Greeley first showed Bishop McManus how much Catholics lag behind Protestants in their giving, the bishop had a ready answer: Naturally, it's their lower socioeconomic status. Catholics, historically immigrants, have always been below Protestants (and especially mainline Protestants) in their incomes, and low giving is merely a reflection of their lower incomes. Not so, Father Greeley informed him. While this may have been true at one time, Catholics have made great economic strides in the postwar years, so that today the annual household income of Catholics is virtually the same as that of mainline Protestants.

Bishop McManus's second explanation concerned the cost of Catholic schools. Parents making the financial sacrifice by paying tuition in order to send their children to parochial schools naturally had less left over to place in the collection basket each Sunday. Again, Father Greeley refuted the argument. His figures showed that parents who sent their children to parochial schools actually contributed at higher levels than the average Catholic family. With these two obvious explanations not working, what were the causes?

Greeley's own explanation was controversial. It was alienation, he claimed. The laity were alienated from the Church hierarchy over a number of issues, the most important of which had to do with the Church's teachings on sexual ethics. Church teachings on birth control, which had been widely promulgated in the late 1960s to early 1970s, had angered Catholics. The laity wasn't buying this teaching, and was showing its displeasure by withholding contributions.

Bishop McManus held out for another explanation. He felt that Catholics focused too much on their parish's needs (a parish that was out of debt obviously had less need) and not enough on what they themselves could afford to give. He suggested that Catholics be taught to contribute a portion of their income to their church. Most families, he thought, should be able to contribute two percent of their income, and wealthier households up to four percent.

Other researchers have offered other explanations. Peter Zaleski and Charles Zech (1994), in the study of giving in 201 congregations that was cited above, placed most of the blame for low Catholic giving on parish size, focusing their attention on the larger, more impersonal Catholic parishes. In trying to explain the differences in giving between Catholics and Protestants, they asked "what if?" Catholics were like Protestants with respect to their socioeconomic status, parish size, and religious attitudes. How would these hypothetical changes impact Catholic giving? They concluded that "reducing Catholic parish size would be the one action having the greatest impact on giving."

In a different study using the same data, Zaleski and Zech (1995) found that Catholic parishes located in regions where Catholics are a minority receive larger contributions than parishes in areas where Catholics constitute a majority of the population. They concluded that parishes that face more competition from other religions are forced to "compete" and are more responsive to parishioners' needs, which in turn results in more generous contributions. Parishes that have a "monopoly" status in that Catholics are the dominant religious group in their region lack these competitive pressures, may be less responsive to parishioners' needs, and thus receive lower contributions.

Like Bishop McManus, John and Sylvia Ronsvale (1995) have focused their analysis on cost differentials between operating a Catholic parish and a Protestant congregation. They've found that in many cases giving follows costs. That is, people give enough to pay the bills. They speculate that the low compensation paid to Catholic clergy, compared to their Protestant counterparts, combined with the larger size of Catholic parishes (more members to support each priest), explains why Catholics give less.

A popular explanation for low Catholic giving emphasizes the laity's dissatisfaction with the amount of participation that they're allowed in church decision-making in general, and with regard to church finances in particular. Frank Butler, director of Foundations and Donors Interested in Catholic Activities (FADICA) was quoted in the 1990 *National Catholic Reporter* article that was cited above. Dr. Butler expressed concern over the Church's lack of accountability: "A concern of many Catholics is the clerical control of money and accountability, openness. People are much more willing today to ask questions about how money is being used."

That same article raised another theory for low Catholic giving — the perception that the Church is actually quite wealthy. This is a variation of the arguments made by Bishop McManus and the Ronsvales, that Catholics tie their giving to the costs of running the Church. The article quotes Covington Kern, secretary-treasurer of the Diocesan Fiscal Management Conference: "We don't have some deep, hidden well of cash like Fort Knox. But people perceive that because of (church) buildings."

Father Thomas Sweetser (1991), the widely respected founder and co-director of the Parish Evaluation Project, gave his opinion on why Catholic giving is low, based on his consulting experience and surveys. He cited 19 reasons. They included a variation of Greeley's theory of alienation; the belief by many Catholics that the Church really doesn't need the money; and concerns over accountability. But he also added two others. One is the pastor's leadership style, which he argues must be participative and inclusive. The other is that Catholics lack a tradition of planned giving. They are accustomed to giving through weekly offertory collections, and the amounts may depend on how much is available in their checkbook that week. They may not even know how much they've given during the year, or how their giving corresponds to parish expenses.

Jim Castelli (1994), a free-lance author who frequently writes on Catholic issues, offered six suggestions for increasing Catholic contributions. They included ideas set forth by others, such as keeping the laity informed on how the money is spent, and the importance of pastors, demonstrating a participative leadership style. He also noted the poor job most seminaries do in training priests in financial management. But he concluded by observing, "When all is said and done, the money crisis facing the Catholic Church is more than a money problem. It's a symptom of larger problems: the decline of community and the confusion about purpose. The way to raise more money for the church is to become better at being a church."

Monsignor Timothy Collins (1996), a pastor in the Archdiocese of New York, probably articulated the silent belief of many when he expressed the opinion that the problem is church mismanagement, not the lack of money: "Talk to the priests in dioceses where the finances are mismanaged and the structures of the church neglected. Almost every priest can detail waste and foolishness; many can articulate the hopelessness that such neglect begets."

One approach that has been shown not to increase contributions is the sponsorship of fund-raising activities like bingo. Dean Hoge and Boguslaw Augustyn (1997) examined data collected from 1,682 parishes by the Educational Testing Service as part of its National Survey of Catechists and Religious Education. Among their conclusions were that "use of regular fund-raising programs such as bingo is associated with lower giving. Either the programs themselves, or the parish cultures which underlie such programs somehow discourage giving" (p. 58).

The U.S. Catholic Bishops had the opportunity to place their mark on the giving issue when they, through the U.S. Catholic Conference, issued a pastoral letter in late 1992 titled "Stewardship: A Disciple's Response." This letter, five years in its development, was expected by many to provide some practical guidance for those in the trenches who are fighting the Church's financial battles. Instead, the bishops opted for a theologically based treatise on the importance of stewardship. They failed to provide any specific recommendations or policies to increase giving. Some praised the bishops for having taken this high road, and for choosing to focus on the total stewardship message of proper use of time, talent, and treasure, rather than just focusing on the money issue. Others expressed frustration that the bishops had ducked the hard questions of putting their theology into practice. They said nothing about better fund-raising and increased accountability on their part as to where the money goes.

A Word on Defining Religious Giving

Religious giving can be viewed in essentially two ways. One, a narrow definition, considers contributions made to the parish. These include funds that are meant to support the parish directly, as well as those that are merely collected by the parish acting as the agent for the larger Church. The former include contributions to support current operations and those that are part of a parish-wide capital campaign. The latter include giving for causes like Catholic Charities, the U.S. Bishops Campaign for Human Development, and Peter's Pence.

A broader view of religious giving includes any giving resulting from a religious motivation, even if the money is donated to an organization that's not explicitly religious. Examples would include the Red Cross or Habitat for Humanity. Many Catholics contribute to these and similar causes because they believe that it's their Christian duty to support the work of these organizations. Contributions to Catholic colleges and universities would also fit into this category.

This book uses the narrow view of religious giving. It tends to be more precise, since it doesn't require us to speculate on the motive for giving as the broader definition does. We tried to capture a sense of the broader definition when we asked our respondents about their giving to religious and non-religious groups outside the denomination. Later in this book we examine the extent to which giving to the parish is affected by this broader giving.

Stewardship Versus Fund-raising

The study of religious contributions really embraces two separate but related issues. The first is stewardship: returning to God a portion of the bounty that God has given us, making us aware that everything in our life is a gift from God. The second is fund-raising: taking care of the financing of the Church as an institution, recognizing that someone has to pay the bills if we want all of the programs and services, both sacramental and non-sacramental, that Catholics believe to be essential components of their religious life. While there is some tension between the two, both have a legitimate place in the discussion of church finances.

The emphasis on stewardship is relatively recent in the Catholic Church. It's really a post-Vatican II phenomenon. Stewardship stresses motivations for giving, rather than methods. While we can find references to stewardship in the Hebrew Scriptures, it received special emphasis in Jesus' parables. The steward is the household supervisor, responsible to the master for maintaining the master's assets. The analogy, of course, is that we humans don't own the world. God owns the world. We are merely God's servants in maintaining the world. Everything we have comes from God. We are to return a portion of our time, talent, and treasure to God as an expression of our thankfulness for all of God's blessings.

Stewardship is essentially a theological understanding of a total way of life. It is a means for lifting the discussion of money to a spiritual level.

Fund-raising, on the other hand, is much more pragmatic. It is concerned with meeting the Church's budgetary requirements. Its message is one of supporting current parish programs and future aspirations. Its focus is on the parish's need to receive, rather than the individual's need to give.

We should be careful not to overstate the differences between stewardship and fund-raising. There is a somewhat fuzzy boundary between the two. Many advocates of stewardship are not averse to using the pragmatic tools of fund-raisers. Likewise, those whose primary concern is with raising money to support the parish programs they cherish often aren't shy about incorporating the language of stewardship. For example, both might legitimately work at helping parishioners see the connection between raising money to purchase a new organ and their personal relationship with God. In fact, some laity have been known to be cynical about the introduction of stewardship in their parishes, viewing it as just another way of raising money.

In this book we examine both: issues that primarily fall in the realm of stewardship, and those that might more commonly be viewed as fund-raising. We also consider other factors affecting giving that probably lie more in the category of "pre-conditions" necessary for Catholics to respond to either a stewardship or fund-raising message.

A Word About Statistics

The results of this study are grounded in sound social-science statistical methodology. Yet, we recognize that most of the readers of this book are not interested in sophisticated statistical methodology. Therefore explanations of the advanced statistics have been omitted. But in the book there are occasional references to some basic statistical concepts. The most important of these is "statistical significance."

Social scientists worry that sometimes the observed relationships between two factors might have occurred by chance, or accident. Before we draw any conclusions, we want to make sure that there is as small a likelihood as possible that the relationship we're observing is accidental. In other words, we want to make sure that the relationship is "significant," that is, not a result of accident or chance, and that it will likely occur again in the future. The criterion that most social scientists use is a 5% or less probability that the relationship they're observing happened by chance. In other words, they're at least 95% certain that it is real and stable, not the result of an accident. There are complex mathematical formulas that allow us to determine the probability that an occurrence is the result of chance. When those formulas indicate that there is less than a 5% probability that the relationship that we've observed is the result of chance, we say the relationship is "statistically significant." The reader can assume that the relationships reported in this book are statistically significant unless we state otherwise.

The Plan of This Book

It's clear from this brief review that observers have suggested a lot of theories trying to explain low Catholic giving, and what can be done about it. The purpose of this book is to sort through these theories and opinions and separate the reality from the myths. Unlike the bishops' letter, this book is meant to be practical, not theological. It will examine religious giving from a variety of viewpoints, offering recommendations on what can and should be done.

The focus of the analysis in this book will be the data collected for the Lilly Endowment-sponsored American Congregational Giving Study. This was a study of giving in five U.S. denominations: Assemblies of God, Southern Baptists, the Evangelical Lutheran Church of America, Presbyterians, and Roman Catholics. Chapter Two will provide some description of the methodology and general results from that study.

Chapters Three through Six will examine four types of influences on Catholic religious giving. The first of these will be the personal characteristics of parishioners (age, income, etc.). The impact of each of these characteristics on religious giving will be discussed (Chapter Three). Next, we will consider how personal religious beliefs of church members influence their giving (Chapter Four). Chapter Five will examine the relationship between denominational policies and programs and parishioners' willingness to contribute. Chapter Six will consider the effect of parish-level factors.

One of the most interesting phenomena in the Church today is the differences among different generations of Catholics (see Davidson et al., 1997). Studies have shown that young Catholics (the so-called "Generation X") differ dramatically from older Catholics in their beliefs. Earlier studies had shown significant differences between baby boomers and the generation that had preceded them. Chapter Seven will summarize some of these differences and examine the effect they have on giving patterns across these generations.

The final chapter is titled "Seven Things the Catholic Church Can Do to Increase Contributions." It will summarize the findings of Chapters Three through Seven, and recommend some practical actions that the U.S. Catholic Church should consider if it hopes to increase members' contributions.

References

Castelli, Jim. "Six Ways the Church Can Raise the Money It Needs," *U.S. Catholic*, August, 1994, pp. 6-13.

Collins, Msgr. Timothy S. "Churches, Schools, Survival, and Money: A Pastor Reflects," *Commonweal*, September 13, 1996, pp. 26-28.

Davidson, James D., Andrea S. Williams, Richard A. Lamanna, Jan Stenftenagel, Kathleen Maas Weigert, William J. Whalen, and Patricia Whittberg, S.C.. *The Search for Common Ground: What Unites and Divides American Catholics*. Huntington, IN: Our Sunday Visitor Publishing, 1997.

Greeley, Andrew and William McManus. *Catholic Contributions: Sociology and Policy*. Chicago: Thomas More Press, 1987.

Harris, Joseph Claude. *The Cost of Catholic Parishes and Schools*. Kansas City: Sheed & Ward, 1996.

_____. "U.S. Catholic Contributions — Up or Down?" *America*, May 21, 1994, pp. 14-16.

Hodgkinson, Virginia A. and Murray S. Weitzman. *Giving and Volunteering in the United States: Findings from a National Survey, 1994 Edition*. Washington, DC: Independent Sector.

_____. *Giving and Volunteering in the United States: Findings from a National Survey, 1992 Edition*. Washington, DC: Independent Sector.

_____. *Giving and Volunteering in the United States: Findings from a National Survey, 1990 Edition*. Washington, DC: Independent Sector.

_____. *Giving and Volunteering in the United States: Findings from a National Survey, 1988 Edition*. Washington, DC: Independent Sector.

Hoge, Dean R. and Boguslaw Augustyn. "Financial Contributions to Catholic Parishes: A Nationwide Study of Determinants," *Review of Religious Research*, Vol. 39, No. 1 (September, 1997), pp. 46-60.

Hoge, Dean R. and Fenggang Yang. "Determinants of Religious Giving in American Denominations: Data From Two Nationwide Surveys," *Review of Religious Research*, Vol. 36, No. 2, (December, 1994), pp. 123-48.

Ronsvale, John and Sylvia. *The State of Church Giving Through 1993.* Champaign, IL: empty tomb, inc.,1995.

Sweetser, Thomas P. "The Money Crunch: Why Don't Catholics Give More?" *Chicago Studies*, Vol. 30, No 1 (April, 1991), pp. 99-111.

Windsor, Pat. "Rising Costs, Low Contributions Spell Red Ink for U.S. Dioceses," *National Catholic Reporter*, February 2, 1990, pp. 3-5.

Zaleski, Peter A. and Charles E. Zech. "Economic and Attitudinal Factors in Catholic and Protestant Religious Giving," *Review of Religious Research*, Vol. 36, No. 2 (December, 1994), pp. 158-67.

Zaleski, Peter A. and Charles E. Zech. "The Effect of Religious Market Competition on Church Giving," *Review of Social Economy*, Vol. 53, No. 3 (Fall, 1995), pp. 350-67.

2
The American Congregational Giving Study

The Catholic Church is not the only denomination concerned about the financial support that its members are providing. The mainline Protestant churches, in addition to their anxieties over declining membership, are troubled by many of their members' unwillingness to pledge. Evangelical Protestants, who teach the tithe as an integral part of their religious doctrine, worry because many of their members are not tithers. It seems that no church is entirely satisfied with the financial support that it receives from its members. For this reason, the Lilly Endowment of Indianapolis, Indiana, in late 1992 commissioned a nationwide study of giving in U.S. churches, which came to be known as The American Congregational Giving Study. Four researchers were enlisted to undertake this study. Dean Hoge, a Presbyterian layman and a sociologist at Catholic University, led the team. He was joined by Michael Donahue, a psychologist who at that time was employed by Search Institute, a Minneapolis-based consulting firm; Patrick McNamara, also a sociologist, from the University of New Mexico; and Charles Zech, an economist from Villanova University.

In early 1993, the research team set about conducting a nationwide survey of U.S. churches and church members in order to learn more about religious giving. Their efforts culminated in a book, *Money Matters: Personal Giving in American Churches*, which was published by Westminster/ John Knox Press in 1996. That book was primarily concerned with learning about the basic factors influencing religious giving in general. This book uses the data collected for that study, and the lessons learned from it, to analyze religious giving only in the Catholic Church.

How the American Congregational Giving Study Was Done

The research team focused its attention on five U.S. religious denominations. Along with the Catholic Church, two relatively high-giving evangelical churches, the Assemblies of God and the Southern Baptist Convention, were included in the study. Two medium-giving mainline Protestant denominations, the Presbyterian Church and the Evangelical Lutheran Church of America, were also selected.

The team decided to study 125 parishes in each denomination, chosen across the nine U.S. census regions. Church membership is uneven, with many small parishes and a few large ones in each denomination. While most parishes are small, most members belong to the large ones. For this reason, the team elected to oversample large parishes, with half of the sample coming from the largest third of the parishes in the region. Otherwise, the sample of churches was random, and was selected by team members, not by denominational officials. Later the bias caused by oversampling the larger parishes was removed by weighting the data.

Field workers personally visited each parish in the sample. Most of the field workers were retired or part-time clergy, or retired church officials. They had two tasks. First, they assisted the pastor (or on occasion, a parish staff member) in the completion of a Congregational Profile (see Appendix A), which summarized the member socioeconomic characteristics, beliefs, and programs in the parish. Sec-

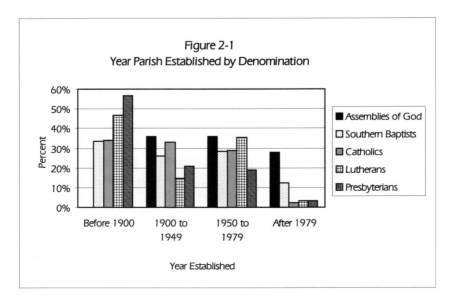

Figure 2-1
Year Parish Established by Denomination

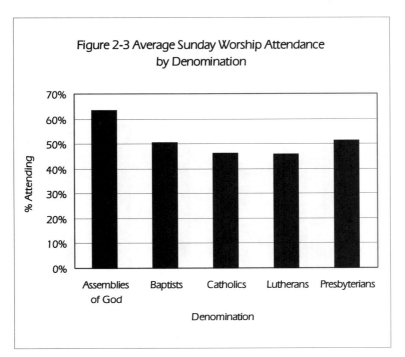

ond, they (not the pastor or staff person) selected a random sample of 30 parish members. Each of these was sent a lay questionnaire, which asked members about their personal beliefs, opinions about both the parish and the denomination, and their personal socioeconomic characteristics (Appendix B). The lay questionnaires were returned directly to the research team, not to the pastor. Overall, 61.2% of the lay questionnaires were returned. The response rate was 55.2% for the Assemblies of God, 53.9% among Southern Baptists, 66.7% for Presbyterians, 70.1% for Lutherans, and 60.5% for Catholics. Because 30 members were surveyed from each parish, regardless of size, a second weighting took place to ensure an appropriate distribution of church members in the sample.

Like most studies of this kind, the individuals who returned the lay questionnaires were not totally representative of the overall church membership. They tended to be more urban, more highly educated, with higher incomes, and more committed to their church, than typical church members. Again, this is common, but any analysis of the lay questionnaires should keep this in mind. Likewise, a few members reported making huge contributions to their church in the last year. Not many households can afford to give $25,000 or more to their church on an annual basis,

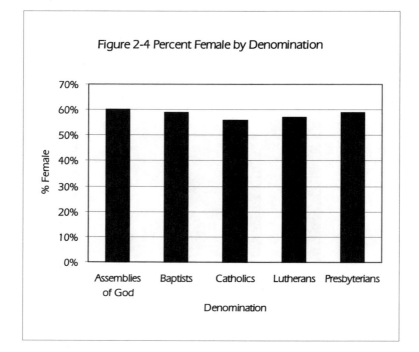

Figure 2-4 Percent Female by Denomination

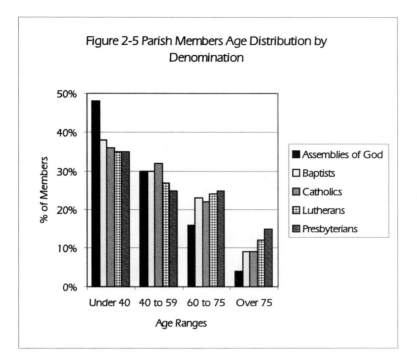

Figure 2-5 Parish Members Age Distribution by Denomination

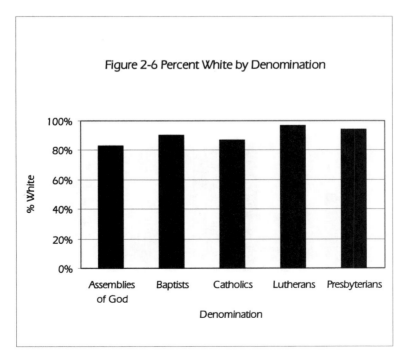

Figure 2-6 Percent White by Denomination

but some members of our sample did. These were most likely one-time gifts, and not indicative of overall giving patterns. Social scientists typically drop these "outliers" from the sample, if there aren't too many of them, and that's what we did.

As a check on its sampling, the research team also commissioned a Gallup telephone survey of U.S. church members. Because of the difficulty in collecting an adequate sample from the smaller denominations in the study, the

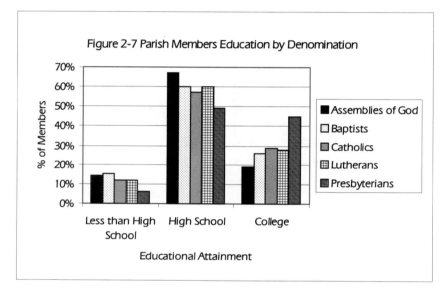

Figure 2-7 Parish Members Education by Denomination

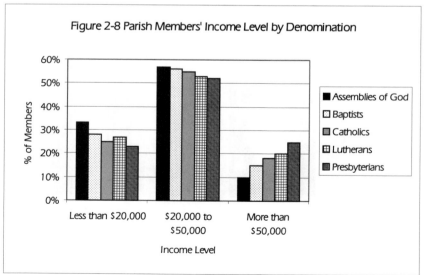

Figure 2-8 Parish Members' Income Level by Denomination

Gallup survey included only people who said they were Baptists, Lutherans, or Catholics. The Gallup survey asked the same questions that had been asked on the lay questionnaire, except that it also included questions on matters of sexual ethics that Andrew Greeley had found to be so important in explaining the decline in Catholic contributions.

Finally, after all of the data had been collected, the researchers interviewed a number of pastors and lay leaders. These interviews resulted in a variety of quotes that were rich in insights and understanding of Church and put a human face on the raw data.

Description of the Parishes in the Sample

What did the Catholic parishes look like? How were they different from the Protestant churches? Remember, these are the characteristics of the parishes as a whole, not of the sample of members who completed the lay questionnaire.

Size and Age Characteristics of the Parishes

Figures 2-1 through 2-3 summarize some of the descriptive characteristics of the churches in our sample. They show that Catholic

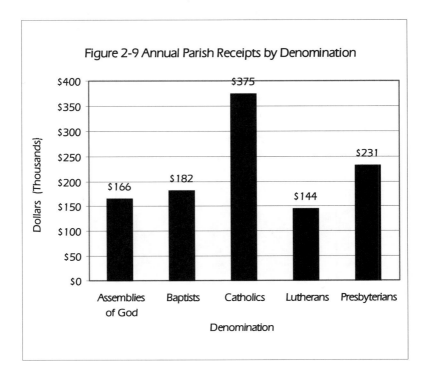

Figure 2-9 Annual Parish Receipts by Denomination

parishes in our sample tended to be about middle-aged, compared to the mainline Protestant churches, which are older, and the evangelical churches, which are younger. Catholic parishes were by far the largest (almost eight times larger than the average Protestant church in our sample). Surprisingly, in spite of the Catholic Church's historic emphasis on Sunday Mass attendance, Catholic parishes had the second lowest percent of their members attending weekly services, barely edging out the Lutherans.

Parish Members' Characteristics

Figures 2-4 through 2-8 summarize the member demographic characteristics of the parishes in our sample. The Catholic parishes were similar to the Protestant congregations in their gender distribution and were about in the middle in the age distribution of their members. Like the Protestant parishes in the sample, the Catholic parishes were overwhelmingly white. Neither the education distribution nor the income distribution of the members of the Catholic parishes in our sample differed remarkably from those of the sample's Protestant congregations.

Parish Finances

The receipts that the parishes in the sample received from various sources are shown in Figures 2-9 through 2-11. As one might expect, Catholic parishes, since they're much larger than the Protestant parishes in our sample, had the largest amount of total receipts. But, as

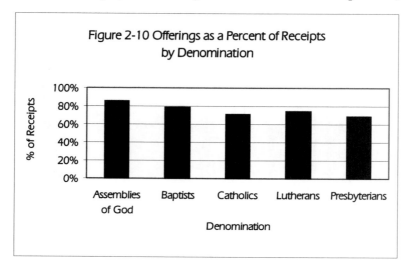

Figure 2-10 Offerings as a Percent of Receipts by Denomination

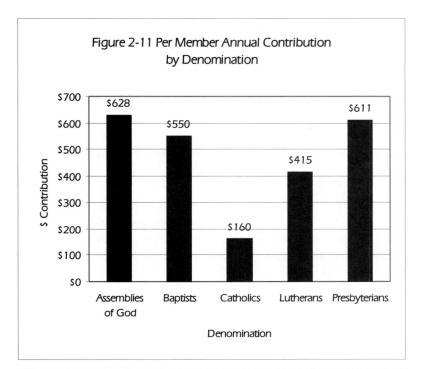

Figure 2-11 Per Member Annual Contribution by Denomination

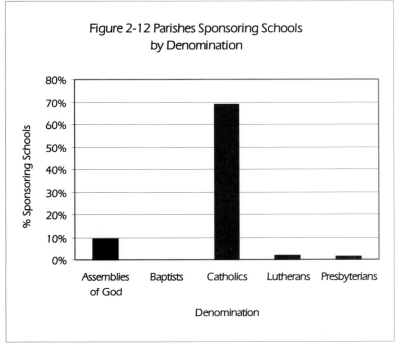

Figure 2-12 Parishes Sponsoring Schools by Denomination

Figure 2-10 demonstrates, next to Presbyterians, Catholics were least likely to rely on regular offerings to support their church. The remainder of their budget was met by heavy reliance on special offerings, fund-raisers (bingo?), and a variety of other sources, including income earned from investments and income generated by renting out parish facilities. Figure 2-11 shows, just as every other study on the topic has shown, that Catholic parishioners in our sample contributed far less to their church than did the Protestants in our sample.

Parish Programs

The types of programs offered in the parishes in our sample are shown in Figures 2-12 to 2-15. As might be expected, Catholic parishes were more likely to sponsor a parochial school, either on their own or in collaboration with another parish. Surprisingly, the Catholic parishes in our sample were also the most likely to sponsor a day-care center or preschool, and most likely to sponsor a latchkey program.

Almost every parish in our sample offered religious education (CCD, Sunday School) for children, and the vast majority also sponsored these programs for their youth. Catholics were well behind the Protestants

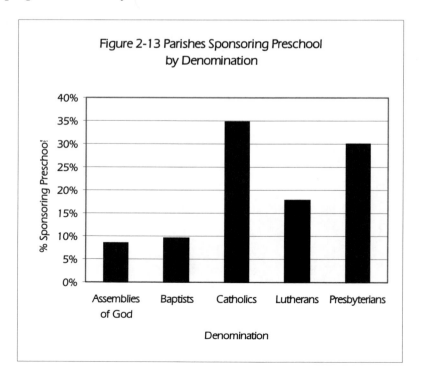

Figure 2-13 Parishes Sponsoring Preschool by Denomination

in our sample in their offering of adult religious education. Catholics also tended to lag behind in their offering of prayer or study groups, but they were comparable to the Protestants in the sample in their offerings of adult special-interest groups, providing more of some, but less of others.

Summary

This chapter has provided a brief summary of the American Congregational Giving Study and a description of the sample of parishes that comprised the study. The rest of this book is concerned with our findings from investigating the Catholic parishes and laity in our sample. But from time to time, to put our findings in perspective, they will be compared to the Protestants that we studied. Oftentimes the Catholics in our sample give their Church a lower rating on issues of concern than do the Protestants. Where this occurs, we simply point it out. We leave it to the reader to decide if a low rating in some categories is truly warranted, and whether in each particular case a low rating is a good thing or a bad thing.

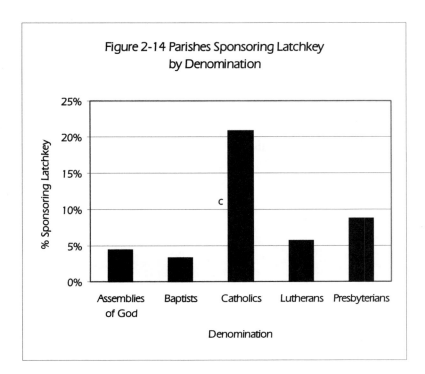

Figure 2-14 Parishes Sponsoring Latchkey by Denomination

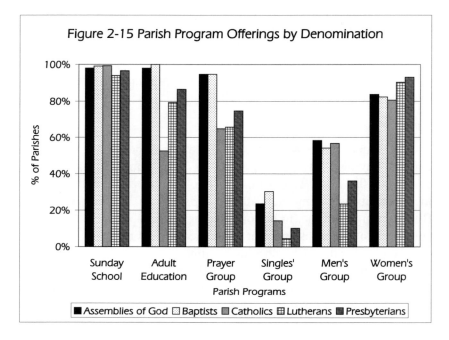

Figure 2-15 Parish Program Offerings by Denomination

References

Dean R. Hoge, Charles E. Zech, Patrick McNamara, and Michael J. Donahue. *Money Matters: Personal Giving in American Churches.* Louisville: Westminster/John Knox, 1996.

Readers interested in a more thorough explanation of methodology involved in collecting the data for this study should consult: Dean R. Hoge, Charles E. Zech, Patrick McNamara, and Michael J. Donahue. *Research Report on the American Congregational Giving Study*, Life Cycle Institute, The Catholic University of America, 1995. The Report can be found in the libraries of Catholic University, The University of New Mexico, and Villanova University.

3

Personal Parishioner Characteristics

This brief chapter considers myths and realities concerning the effect of parishioners' personal characteristics on their religious giving. How do people's income level, age, race, and so on affect their contributions to the Church? It could be concluded that these factors, while of interest, are really outside of the Church's control and therefore carry no policy implications. On the other hand, to the extent that the Church can target its message and programs, it's important that it knows about the giving patterns of people with different personal characteristics. For example, if it can be shown that people with high incomes have a different giving pattern than other parishioners, or respond to different giving messages, then a parish with a large number of high earners should be able to take advantage of that information to target that group. The same may be true for a parish with a large number of unmarried members, or a parish with a substantial minority population, and so on. This chapter investigates the giving levels associated with various personal characteristics.

There is a close relationship between people's personal characteristics and their income. A household's income level is so important that it overshadows the effects of other characteristics on its contributions. In recognition of this problem, this chapter views religious contributions both from the perspective of the dollar amounts and the percent of household income that is contributed.

Income

Every study has found income to be an important factor in explaining people's religious contributions. Basically, dollar contributions increase as people's incomes rise. Households with more income can afford to contribute more. Our data agrees with this pattern. Figure 3-1 divides our sample into six income-categories. Households in higher income-categories contribute more. The only exception is a blip among middle-income classifications, where households in the $35,000- to $50,000-income range contribute more than those earning $50,000 to $75,000. But the overall pattern is apparent.

Households with more income contribute more to the Church. But does the increase in contributions increase at the same rate as income? Does one household that earns twice as much income as another household contribute twice as much? Most of the research on this question has concluded that the answer is no. Contributions increase as household incomes increase, but at a slower rate. Upper-income households contribute more dollars than do lower-income households, but they contribute a lower *percentage* of their income. Our findings are shown in Figure 3-2, where we compare the percentage of income contributed across the six income-categories. Here we see a generally decreasing pattern (again with that blip among lower middle-income households). Higher-income households contribute far less, as a portion of their income, than do lower-income households. In fact, those households earning more than $100,000

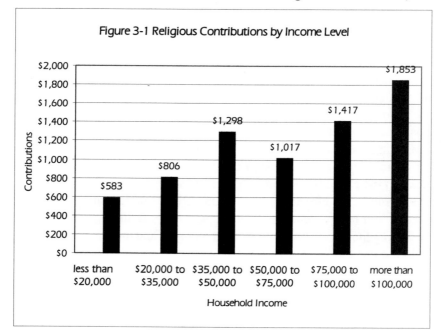

Figure 3-1 Religious Contributions by Income Level

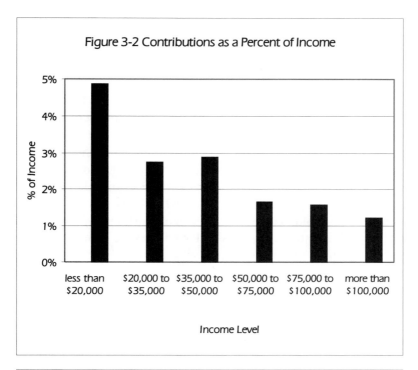

Figure 3-2 Contributions as a Percent of Income

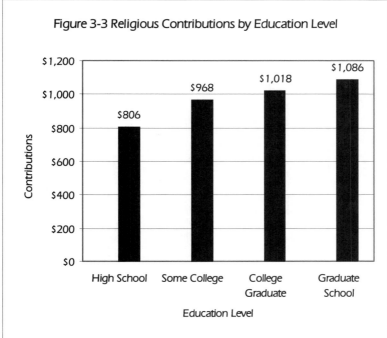

Figure 3-3 Religious Contributions by Education Level

contribute only about one-fourth as much of their income as those earning less than $20,000.

In *Money Matters* we found a similar pattern for the Protestants in our sample. Higher-income Protestants also gave a lower percent of their income. But the decrease wasn't as dramatic as it was for Catholics. There are generally two explanations set forth to account for this pattern. One is that households view their contributions to the church as containing two elements. The first component is to pay their "fair share" of parish membership. This figure would be a constant dollar figure for all households, regardless of their income. The second element contains a "proportion of income" component, whereby people recognize that wealthier households should contribute a proportionately larger share of their income. Combining these two elements results in the observed pattern: as a household's income increases, dollar contributions increase (because of the proportion of income component) but not at the same rate as income has increased (because the fixed, fair-share component has not changed).

The other explanation is that households base their contributions on the level of income that they *expect* to receive in a particular time pe-

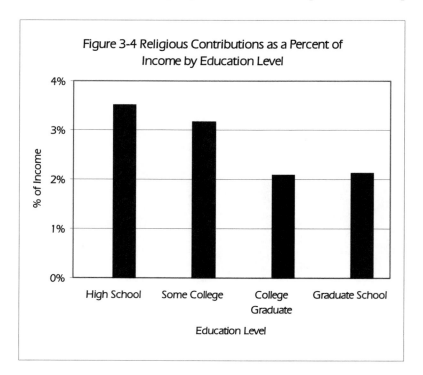

Figure 3-4 Religious Contributions as a Percent of Income by Education Level

riod. Sometimes their expectations are wrong, and they actually earn more money than they thought they would. But none of this unanticipated increase in income is contributed to the church, so if their income has unexpectedly increased, contributions as a percent of income will decrease.

In any event, all churches, including the Catholic Church, have a big job ahead of them in instilling a sense of stewardship among their wealthiest members.

Education

Just as people with greater incomes contribute more to the Church, so too, studies have shown that more highly educated people contribute more. This is not surprising, since education is typically associated with greater earning power. However, when looking at the *trend* in giving, Greeley found that when he measured giving by the percent of income contributed, the decrease was far greater for more highly educated Catholics than for those with less education. From 1963 to 1984, contributions as a percent of income decreased from 2.4% to 1.3% for those who went to college, compared to a decrease from 2.0% to 1.3% for those who did not graduate from high school. Greeley attributed this sharper decline among more educated Catholics to their greater dissatisfaction with the

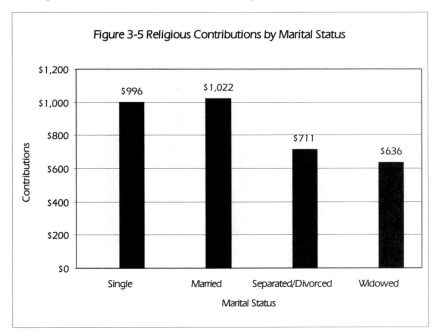

Figure 3-5 Religious Contributions by Marital Status

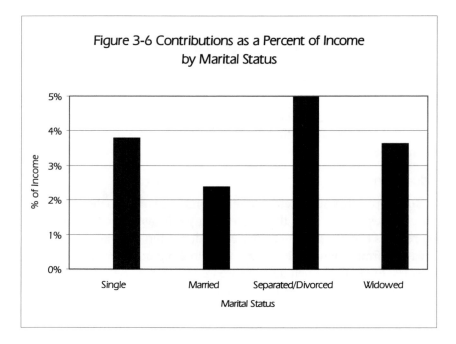

Figure 3-6 Contributions as a Percent of Income by Marital Status

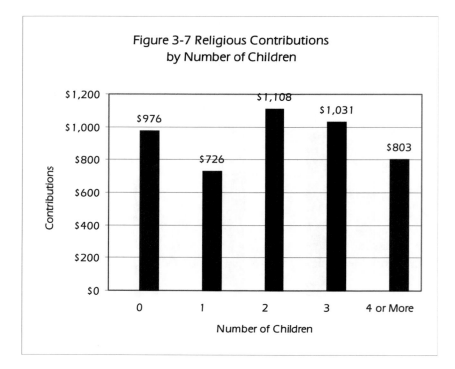

Figure 3-7 Religious Contributions by Number of Children

Church's authoritarian structure and moral stances (Greeley and McManus, 1987, pp. 40-41, 44).

Our data did not allow the identification of any trends. But, as Figure 3-3 shows, Catholics with more education contributed more. At the same time our results support Greeley's contention that more highly educated Catholics contribute a lower percentage of their income. Figure 3-4 shows that on a percent-of-income basis Catholics with a college degree or more contribute only about two-thirds as much as those without a college degree. The premise that this pattern is caused by greater dissatisfaction with the denomination is tested later in this book. But we can note here that the findings are inconclusive.

Race

Most studies have shown that whites contribute more to their churches than do racial minorities. This has been partially attributed to their generally higher levels of income. So as with other personal characteristics, the analysis of giving patterns by race must consider both actual dollars contributed as well as the percent of income.

We found no difference at all in the dollar contributions between whites and non-whites (there were too few non-whites in our sample to allow for a more detailed breakdown of racial minorities). Likewise, there was no significant difference between them when giving was measured by the percent of income. For Catholics, minorities do not contribute at any different levels than do whites. In *Money Matters* we found a similar pattern for the Protestant denominations that we studied. Race is apparently not a consideration in determining religious contributions.

Family Status

Researchers all agree that married people contribute more than do single, separated, widowed, or divorced church members. Several reasons have been suggested. One is that it may be the result of higher incomes for married couples, many of whom have two wage-earners. Another explanation is that churches don't do an adequate job in getting their unmarried members involved. Most churches offer a variety of programs for children, such as a parochial school or CCD, CYO, youth choirs, sponsoring Scout troops, etc. Parents naturally get involved. But in many parishes the program offerings that appeal to unmarried members are sparse.

In Figure 3-5 we can see that married households contribute significantly more than do widowed and separated/divorced Catholics, but only slightly more than single parishioners. But from Figure 3-6 we can see that this is partially a result of these households' higher incomes. Based on the percentage of their income contributed, married couples contribute significantly *less* than do other parish households.

Apart from income, does the existence of children in a family make a difference? What about the myth that since many parish programs are geared toward children, having children in the home leads to more attachment to the parish, and thus larger contributions? The answer here is mixed. From Figure 3-7 we can conclude that households with two or three children under the age of 18 living at home contribute more than do other households. But smaller families (one child at home) and larger families (four or more children at home) contribute less than do families with no children living at home. And Figure 3-8 reveals that households with no children contribute a larger portion of their income to the Church. So the reality is that higher incomes, rather than parish attachment, brought about by their children's participation, explains the higher giving levels of married households.

What about the religious preference of a spouse? Do households where both the husband and wife are Catholics contribute more than a house-

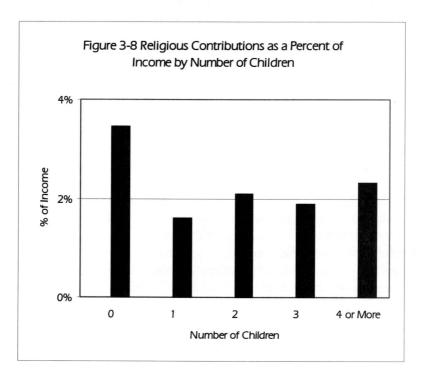

Figure 3-8 Religious Contributions as a Percent of Income by Number of Children

hold where one of the parties is not a Catholic? One would probably think so, if attachment to the parish is enhanced by both partners sharing the same faith. But the reality is that it doesn't make any difference. We found that married households where both partners are Catholic do not contribute more (in fact, they actually contribute slightly less) than do households where one of the spouses is not Catholic, although the differences are not statistically significant. One explanation might be that Catholics who are married to non-Catholics (who tend to be more generous to their churches) are positively influenced by the example of their spouses.

Some of the family variables (such as being married) are associated with higher religious contributions. The impact of others (such as having children) is erratic. They show no clear pattern of either increasing or decreasing contributions. Still others (such as if one's spouse attends the same church) are unrelated to church giving. At best, then, family status would be considered a weak determinant of religious giving.

Age

A fairly consistent pattern has emerged from studies on religious giving by different age groups. Generally, contributions rise as people get older, peaking in late middle age, and then declining. This pattern has been shown to prevail across denominations. As people get older, they have more discretionary income that they can use for things like religious contributions. But once they retire and begin living on a fixed income, they again have less discretionary income.

While the ebb and flow of discretionary income as people age has no doubt historically been a main factor in explaining the differences in giving by age, recent research has focused on generational differences (see Davidson et al., 1997). According to this theory, the defining moment for Catholics was Vatican II. The Catholic Church today, then, is really composed of three generations: the pre-Vatican II generation; the Vatican II generation; and the post-Vatican II generation. Catholics who came of age prior to Vatican II (essentially those born before and during WWII) were raised in a hierarchical church, where the emphasis was on tradition. When they speak of the Church, they are most likely referring to the magisterium. They tend to regard the Church as an institution, and are more likely to support it financially.

The post-Vatican II generation consists of those who came of age after Vatican II had occurred and most of its reforms had been implemented. They were raised in a Church with a decreased emphasis on

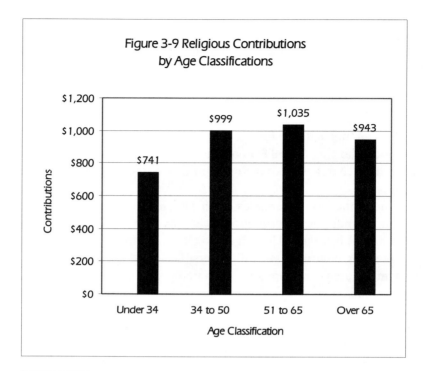

Figure 3-9 Religious Contributions
by Age Classifications

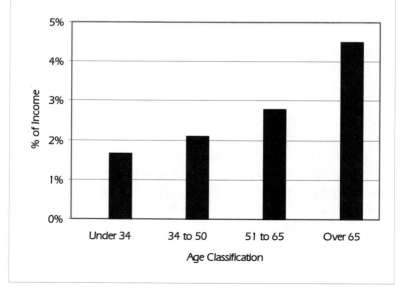

Figure 3-10 Religious Contributions as a Percent of
Income by Age Classification

tradition and an increased emphasis on democratic processes and the primacy of individual conscience. When they think of the Church, they think of it in terms of "the people of God." They have less of an institutional commitment to the Church, and are more reluctant to support it financially.

The Vatican II generation primarily encompasses the baby boomer generation, especially those born before 1960. They are caught in the middle. They came of age during Vatican II and the transition period that followed it. They have one foot in the old church and one foot in the new. Although they may continue some of the devotional practices of the Church that are dear to the hearts of the pre-Vatican II generation, in most attitudes they tend to be more like post-Vatican II Catholics. This includes their attitude toward financial support of the Church.

The impact of these generational differences as possible explanations for any differences in religious contributions are discussed in Chapter Seven. For now, we can recognize that there are differences in giving among these different generations, and the differences reflect the pattern discussed at the beginning of this section. As Figure 3-9 illustrates, religious contributions increase as one moves from the youngest group through the late middle-age group, and then they decline for those 65 or older. Contributions as a percent of income increase uniformly as one moves from the youngest to the oldest age brackets (Figure 3-10). This reality is consistent with the myth that the effect of age on religious contributions depends on the availability of discretionary income during each of the periods of a person's life.

Philanthropy Outside the Parish

We have frequently heard it said that one reason that Catholic giving lags behind that of other denominations is because Catholics are so generous in giving to causes outside their parish. These include donations to their colleges, religiously based organizations like Catholic Charities, and secular causes such as the United Way. But this is a myth that cannot be supported in reality. For one thing, in *Money Matters* we found that Catholics in our sample donated an average of $576 per household to religious and non-religious causes outside their parish. This was the second lowest among the five denominations. Presbyterians were the most generous, contributing an average of $816 per household. Members of the Assembly of God gave an average of $716, while Southern Baptists donated $615, and Lutherans contributed an average of $526 to organizations outside their congregation.

A second reason why this myth can't be supported is that those Catholics who are the most generous in their contributions to causes outside the parish are *also* the largest contributors to their parish. Figure 3-11 shows that Catholics who donate more to organizations outside the parish also contribute more to their parish. This does not support the existence of any trade-off in the minds of Catholics between giving to their parish and donating to other causes. Rather, it shows that whatever generosity exists among Catholics extends to both their parish and to other worthwhile causes. The tendency to be generous to one's parish is closely related to generosity to other charitable causes.

Although the differences are not statistically significant, it should be mentioned that when contributions to the parish are measured as a percent of income the relationship is just the reverse: Catholics' contributions to their parish as a percent of their income decrease when they donate more to other organizations.

From this, we can conclude that low Catholic giving to their churches has nothing to do with generosity to other charitable organizations. That is a myth that cannot be supported in reality.

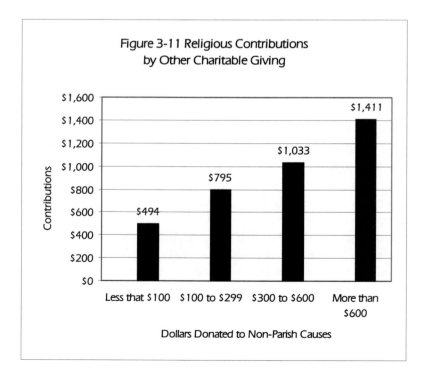

Figure 3-11 Religious Contributions by Other Charitable Giving

Conclusions

From this brief review of the effect of various personal characteristics on Catholic contributions we found two that were strongly related to religious contributions. One, as we had expected, was income. Not only was income itself found to significantly affect religious contributions, but with few exceptions (race being one notable case), personal characteristics that tend to be associated with higher incomes were also associated with higher levels of religious contributions. But while this was the finding when we considered the dollar amounts contributed, the reverse was generally true when we examined the portion of people's incomes that they contributed. High-income households (and people with characteristics associated with higher incomes) gave a lower percentage of their incomes to the Church.

The other strong relationship that we found was between people's donations to charitable causes and organizations outside the parish and their contributions to the parish. Households with larger contributions to other charities also contributed more to their parish. It would not be reasonable to argue that one *causes* the other. Rather, some of the same underlying factors that induce people to be generous in their other philanthropy are also influencing their decision to contribute to the Church.

References

Davidson, James D. et al. *The Search for Common Ground: What Unites and Divides Catholic Americans*. Huntington, IN: Our Sunday Visitor Publishing, 1997.

Greeley, Andrew and William McManus. *Catholic Contributions: Sociology and Policy*. Chicago: The Thomas More Press, 1987.

Hoge, Dean R., Charles E. Zech, Patrick McNamara, and Michael J. Donahue. *Money Matters: Personal Giving in American Churches*, Louisville: Westminster/John Knox, 1996.

4

Religious Beliefs
and Commitment

In the previous chapter we considered the effect of socioeconomic factors on Catholic religious giving. We observed that while the impact of these factors on giving is important to understand, they are generally beyond the Church's control. The best the Church can hope to do is to recognize that different parishioners, for example unmarried parishioners, have different pastoral needs that must be met. Meeting those needs will result in greater satisfaction with the Church. One by-product of this may well be that these members will increase their religious contributions.

This chapter carries a similar theme, in that it examines the effect on giving of factors that the Church is either unwilling or unable to change, but whose effect on giving can serve as a valuable pastoral signal. It is important for the Church to understand the effect of both people's religious beliefs and commitment on their contributions. Not because it would want to change its teachings merely to attract more contributions, but rather because understanding the impact that its teachings may be having on contributions will help the Church to respond pastorally. For example, if Andrew Greeley is correct, and a major reason for low Catholic contributions is alienation over the Church's teaching on issues like birth control, this is important information. It would signal the Church that it hasn't done an adequate job pastorally in explaining its position. Without information like this, the Church may come to believe that everything is fine, and continue on the same path without addressing underlying problems.

This chapter first looks at the impact that some beliefs have on Catholic contributions. Later, we consider the effect of religious commitment on contributions. Are the more religiously committed contributing more, as we would expect? If they're not, we have even a more challenging task ahead of us if we hope to increase Catholic contributions.

Beliefs

Other than Greeley, not many researchers have considered the effect of specific religious beliefs on giving, perhaps because they've concluded that churches are unwilling to modify their teachings merely to attract larger contributions. Those few studies that have looked at the effect of beliefs have always concluded that parishioners with more orthodox beliefs and more conservative attitudes on moral issues contribute more. For example, John Hilke (1980) compared the effect of religious orthodoxy on contributions across a number of Protestant denominations. He found it to have a strong effect on religious giving. Andrew Greeley, in another study that he co-authored with William McCready and Kathleen McCourt (1976), found a moderate relationship between contributions and both people's agreement with Church teachings and their reluctance to criticize priests. Dean Hoge and Fenggang Yang (1994) found that

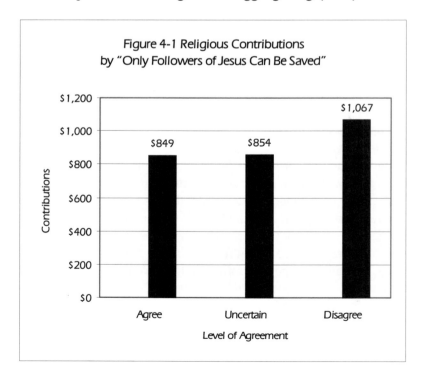

Figure 4-1 Religious Contributions
by "Only Followers of Jesus Can Be Saved"

Catholics who do the following tended to be more generous givers: those who prayed more often, believed in life after death, considered the Bible to be an important guide in making life decisions, regard Church teaching as being an important guide in making life decisions, believe their faith to be free of doubts, and consider pre-marital sex to be always wrong. Another study, by D'Antonio et al. (1989), reported that Catholics who agreed with the Church's position on artificial contraception, abortion, and punishment of dissenting theologians, contributed more. But those who approved of some of the Church's more liberal positions, such as the Bishops' letters on the nuclear-arms race and the economy, and the notion of the preferential option for the poor, also gave more. D'Antonio et al., also looked at the effect of attitudes about Church authority on contributions. They found that parishioners who agree that Church leaders should have the final say on what is morally right or wrong regarding both abortion and birth control contributed more than did others. Those who thought these should be joint decisions between the leadership and members gave the next most. The lowest givers were those who felt that abortion and birth control should be individual decisions.

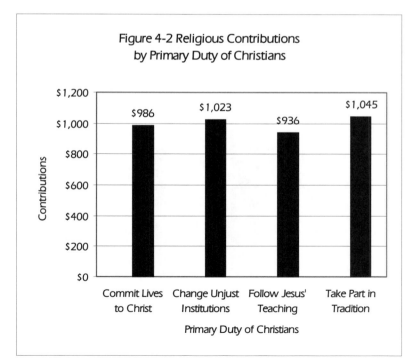

Figure 4-2 Religious Contributions by Primary Duty of Christians

We can conclude from all of this that it is the willingness to accept the Church's official position, and the acknowledgement of its teaching authority, as much as the Church's stance on any one specific issue, that motivates people to contribute more.

In this chapter we consider some beliefs for which the Church may not have taken an official position.

Distinctive Lifestyle Teachings

Researchers who have compared giving patterns across denominations have found higher contributions in so-called "high-tension" churches (Iannaccone, 1994). These are churches that impose demands on their members, such as abstinence from alcohol or certain types of entertainment like movies or dancing, that set them apart from the rest of society. We found this to be true in *Money Matters*. Denominations that place demands on their members that cause them to live a distinctive lifestyle, such as the Assemblies of God and the Southern Baptists, received greater contributions from their members. But this was not true for the Catholic Church. While the Church does not encourage activities such as drinking and gambling, it does not outlaw them, so long as they're done in

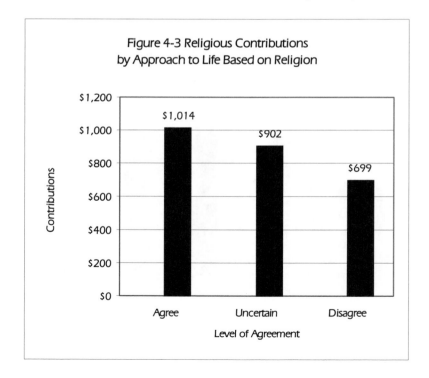

Figure 4-3 Religious Contributions by Approach to Life Based on Religion

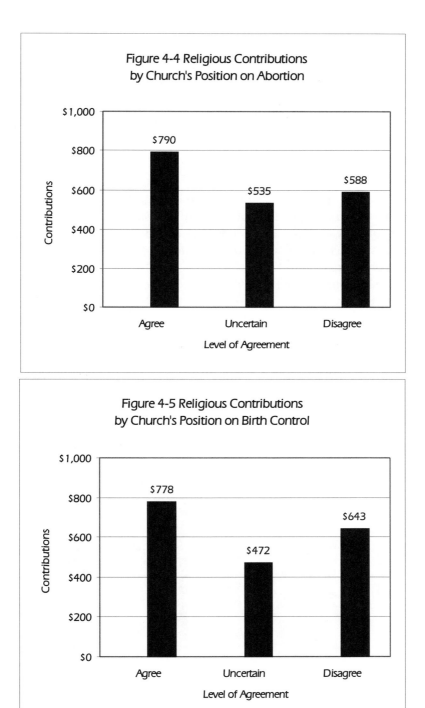

Figure 4-4 Religious Contributions
by Church's Position on Abortion

Figure 4-5 Religious Contributions
by Church's Position on Birth Control

moderation. But some individual pastors do take a harder line on these activities. Do these "high-tension parishes" receive larger contributions? No. Contributions in parishes that claimed to place a special emphasis on teaching abstinence from common societal experiences did not vary significantly from parishes that did not make these demands.

Christian Duty

What about uniquely Christian beliefs? We asked our lay respondents if it is true that only followers of Jesus Christ can be saved. At one time this was a teaching of the Catholic Church. Since Vatican II the Church has backed off this position. Yet 52% of our sample of lay Catholics either agreed with this statement or were uncertain. However, as Figure 4-1 shows, those who disagreed contribute substantially more than the other two groups.

We asked our respondents what they believe to be the primary duty of Christians. Over 60% chose the option, "Following the teachings of Jesus as the basis for spiritual growth." But, as Figure 4-2 illustrates, these were the *lowest givers*. The highest givers were those who responded, "Faithfully participating in the tradition and sacraments of

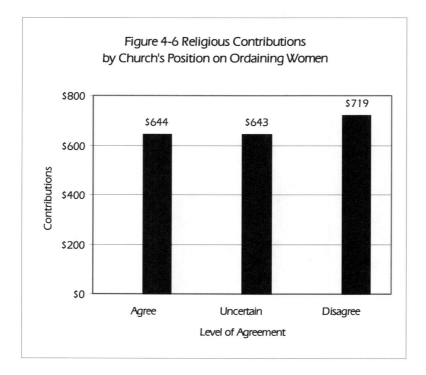

Figure 4-6 Religious Contributions by Church's Position on Ordaining Women

the Church" (22% of the sample) and those (6% of the sample) who selected, "Helping to change unjust social structures." Another 6% chose the response frequently identified with evangelical Christians, "Helping others commit their lives to Christ." This outcome is perplexing. When we think of orthodox beliefs in the Catholic Church, we tend to reflect, as did our sample, on tradition and sacraments, and the importance of Jesus. Yet one of these is associated with high contributions, while the other results in low contributions. A small minority of our respondents believe that their primary duty is to change unjust social structures, which has received relatively less emphasis by the Church. But they are among the better givers. Perhaps these results reflect confusion on the part of parishioners concerning the Church's post-Vatican II message.

Religion in Daily Life

We asked parishioners about the role that religion plays in their daily lives. Almost two-thirds agreed with the statement, "What religion offers me most is comfort in times of trouble and sorrow." But their giving was not significantly different from those who disagreed with that statement or were uncertain. On the other hand, those three-fourths of the respondents who agreed with the statement, "My whole approach to life is based on my religion," contributed significantly more than those who disagreed or were uncertain (Figure 4-3). This is good news for those who make the argument that stewardship, including its financial component, is an essential part of Christian living.

Sexual Ethics

What about Andrew Greeley's contention that it is alienation with the Church's hierarchy over teachings on sexual ethics that is the primary culprit in explaining low Catholic giving? In addition to our congregation profiles and lay survey, we had also contracted with the Gallup Organization to conduct a nationwide survey of church members, including 535 Catholics. Household religious contributions were lower in the Gallup sample than they were in the lay-survey sample. In our Gallup poll we asked about Church teachings on abortion, birth control, and the ordination of women. The sample tended to agree with the Church's position on abortion (54%) and the ordination of women (56%), but disagree with its position on birth control (only 39% agreed). Except for the ordination of women, those who agreed with the Church's position contributed more than those who disagreed or were uncertain, but the differences were not significantly different (Figures 4-4 to 4-6). This finding is consistent with Greeley's hypothesis that parishioners who are angry with the Church over some of its sexual-ethics teachings are giving less. But the relationship is weak, and comes nowhere close to supporting his contention that it is the *primary* explanation for low Catholic giving.

Commitment

Every study of religious giving has found a strong relationship between assorted measures of religious commitment and contributions. This is not to imply that various forms of religious commitment, like Mass attendance or volunteering to serve on parish committees, *cause* parishioners to contribute more. Rather, it is probably an indication that contributing toward the support of their church is simply another way that members play out their religious commitment. The same feelings about their church that induce parishioners to attend daily Mass or volunteer to help clean up the church grounds will probably also cause them to be more generous in supporting their church financially.

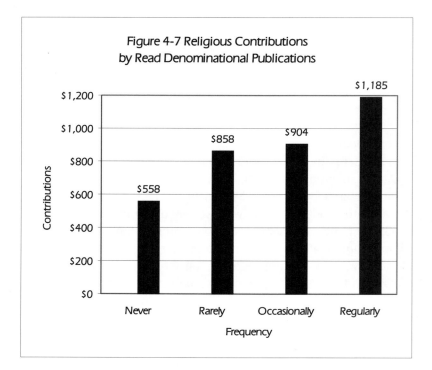

Commitment to the Denomination

When we think of religious commitment, we usually think in terms of commitment to the parish, where the opportunities to demonstrate that commitment are more readily available. Yet, on many criteria, including their reluctance to change religions, Catholics are more committed to their denomination than are most other Christians. We had one measure of their commitment to their denomination. We asked our sample how often they read publications (magazines, newspapers, and newsletters) published by the denomination or diocese. Most of our sample read denominationally sponsored publications either regularly (36%) or occasionally (36%). As shown in Figure 4-7, commitment to the denomination as measured by reading its publications is associated with higher giving.

Commitment to the Parish

We had a variety of measures of commitment to the parish, all of which were significantly related to higher giving. We asked people how long they had been members of the parish (Figure 4-8). Generally, the longer they had been parishioners, the more they gave. Curiously, this

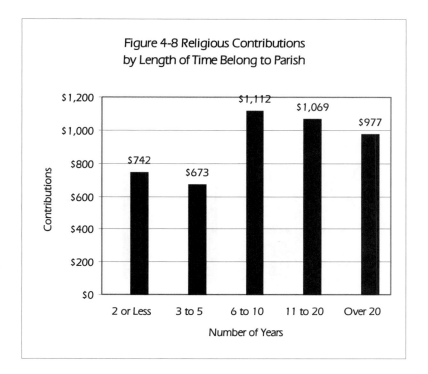

Figure 4-8 Religious Contributions by Length of Time Belong to Parish

was not true at the extremes. New parishioners gave more, and the most senior parishioners gave less, than the overall pattern would have predicted. Low giving on the part of the most senior parishioners might be explained by observing that many of them are probably retired and living on a fixed income, as we discussed in Chapter Three. It's more difficult to understand the high giving on the part of new parishioners. This may be a statistical aberration, since new parishioners made up a small portion of our sample (about 2%). With such a small number of respondents, even one exceptionally large giver in this group could have inflated the average.

What about Mass attendance? Predictably those who attend more frequently also contribute more (Figure 4-9). Likewise, those who attend more non-worship events at their parish also are more generous contributors (Figure 4-10).

In the previous chapter we addressed the myth that one reason Catholics are such poor contributors to their parishes is that they are so generous in supporting other causes. We found that this myth couldn't be supported. Catholics who are more generous to other causes are also more generous to their churches. Another myth is that Catholics perceive a

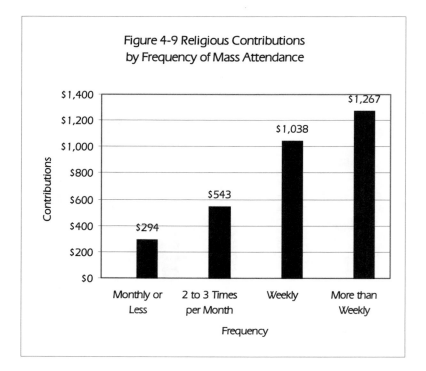

Figure 4-9 Religious Contributions by Frequency of Mass Attendance

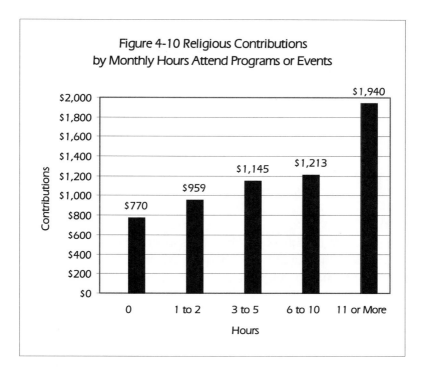

Figure 4-10 Religious Contributions by Monthly Hours Attend Programs or Events

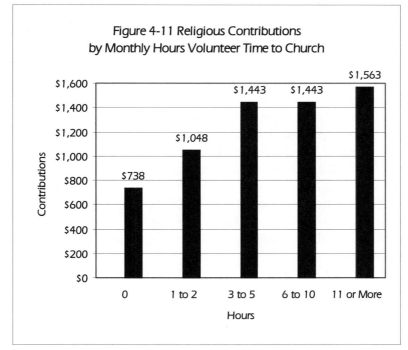

Figure 4-11 Religious Contributions by Monthly Hours Volunteer Time to Church

trade-off among the stewardship components of time, talent, and treasure. We've had plenty of church members tell us of cases where their fellow parishioners found it easy to write a check to support the church, but were unwilling to dig in and contribute their time and talent. We don't doubt that this occurs, but those parishioners are in a minority. As Figure 4-11 illustrates, parishioners who volunteer more time to work in their parish also contribute more dollars. The perceived trade-off between time and dollars doesn't exist. Whatever is motivating church members to express their commitment by contributing their time is also motivating them to contribute their money.

Conclusions

This chapter has considered the effects that religious beliefs and commitment have on religious contributions. We observed that although the acceptance of the Church's beliefs and teachings is an important factor in motivating religious contributions, no one is suggesting that the Church change its teachings merely to raise more money. Yet the way the message is presented and emphasized can be crucial. For example, the Catholic Church teaches that it is important to follow the teachings of Jesus; that it is our obligation to try to change unjust social structures; and that participating in the tradition and the sacraments of the Church are critical. But those parishioners who believe the emphasis should be placed on the latter two of these contribute more than those who emphasize the message of following Jesus. Yet, Jesus would certainly encourage us to change unjust social structures and to participate in the sacraments. Without downplaying the importance of Jesus or changing its fundamental message, the Church might be able to attract more contributions by modifying how it is presented.

One message that the Church need not concern itself with is its teachings on sexual ethics. While our findings support Andrew Greeley in that those who disagree with the Church's position on issues like abortion, birth control, and the ordination of women give less, the relationship is very weak. Certainly we can find no support for asserting that alienation with the hierarchy on these issues is a primary explanation for low Catholic giving.

As expected, we found a strong relationship between contributions and various measures of church commitment, like Mass attendance and reading church-sponsored publications. This doesn't mean that they cause greater contributions, but rather that giving to the church is just another form that religious commitment takes.

It's comforting to know that the more committed church members are also the more generous. But in *Money Matters* we found that the most committed Catholics lag behind the most committed Protestants in their generosity to their church. For example, among those members who attend worship services more than once a week, the average contribution for an Assemblies of God household was $3,510; for Southern Baptists it was $3,416; Presbyterians gave $3,226; and Lutherans $2,840. For Catholics, the figure was $1,267. A similar pattern held for the other commitment measures. In fact, the discrepancy in giving between the Catholics and Protestants in our sample in some cases actually *increased* with their commitment. For example, let us compare Catholics and Lutherans. Among those who only attend services once a month, the average Catholic household contributions were about 60% of those of Lutheran households. But among those who attend more than once a week, Catholic giving was only 45% of Lutheran giving. Priests who speak at Mass about the importance of religious commitment are frequently accused of "preaching to the converted." But while we need to continually affirm our most dedicated church members, we have to impress upon them that they can do better, at least with respect to their financial commitment.

References

D'Antonio, William, James Davidson, Dean Hoge, and Ruth A. Wallace. *American Catholic Laity in a Changing Church*. Kansas City: Sheed & Ward, 1989.

Greeley, Andrew M., William C. McCready, and Kathleen McCourt. *Catholic Schools in a Declining Church*. Kansas City: Sheed & Ward, 1976.

Hilke, John C. "Voluntary Contributions and Monitoring Efforts: Revealed Preference for the Services of Religious Organizations," *Journal for the Scientific Study of Religion*, Vol. 19, No. 2, 1980, pp. 138-45.

Hoge, Dean R. and Fenggang Yang. "Determinants of Religious Giving in American Denominations: Data From Two Nationwide Surveys," *Review of Religious Research*, Vol. 36, No. 2 (December, 1994), pp. 123-48.

Hoge, Dean R., Charles E. Zech, Patrick McNamara, and Michael J. Donahue. *Money Matters: Personal Giving in American Churches*. Louisville: Westminster/John Knox, 1996.

Iannaccone, Laurence R. "Why Strict Churches are Strong," *American Journal of Sociology*, Vol. 99, No. 5 (March, 1994), pp. 1180-1211.

5

Denominational Programs and Processes

Of the many studies that have been conducted on Catholic religious giving, none have considered the effect of the larger Church's programs and decision-making processes (as opposed to their teachings) on parishioners' giving. We can only assume that this neglect is intentional. Maybe it has resulted from researchers' belief that Catholics uniformly love their Church and are unquestionably loyal to its leadership. Or it might be the opposite — maybe they believe that Catholics are frustrated with the hierarchical decision-making structure of the Church and have tuned it out of their own religious contributions decision-making process. Or maybe it reflects their opinion that the programs and processes of the larger Church are simply too distant and not relevant to the everyday lives of most Catholics. Eugene Kennedy (1995), for example, has asserted that an increasing number of Catholics are becoming what he has labeled "Culture Two Catholics." These are devoted Catholics who proclaim their faith through their everyday lives but are totally disinterested in the activities of the Church bureaucracy. Kennedy describes them as "individuals whose Catholicism is internalized."

Whatever the reason, it seems strange that researchers haven't even investigated the question of the role that the larger Church plays in explaining low Catholic contributions. This is especially unusual in light of the findings that the programs and processes of Protestant denominations have been shown to impact their members' giving patterns. For example, alienation with their denomination's programs and processes, as opposed to their teachings, has been shown to be an important factor in explaining the decrease in voluntary contributions that many Protestant congregations have been willing to make to support their denominationally sponsored programs, such as missions (Vallet and Zech, 1995).

For whatever reason, there is a gap in our understanding of the relationship between the programs and processes of the larger Church and members' contributions to their parish. This chapter addresses that gap by considering the effect of Catholic attitudes towards the larger Church's programs, and especially its decision-making processes, on their religious contributions. Throughout this discussion we will be comparing our Catholic samples' opinion on their church's programs and processes with those of our respondents from the four Protestant denominations in our study. It is important to keep in mind that ecclesiastically the Catholic Church is the most hierarchical church in this group.

Denominational Programs

As with most other religions, the vast majority of Catholic church programs are offered at the local, parish level. Preparation for the sacraments, prayer and study groups, ministries in music, evangelization, and church-sponsored social programs are all primarily parish-level activities. Dioceses support parish activities in these areas and others, such as

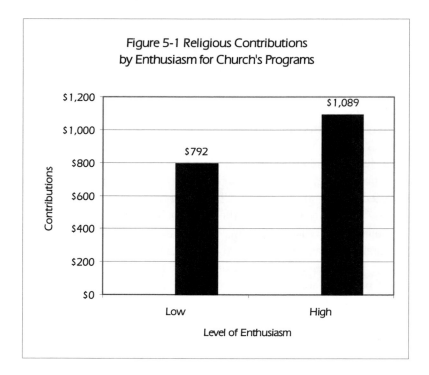

Figure 5-1 Religious Contributions
by Enthusiasm for Church's Programs

parish administration. Dioceses also offer services that at various times impact on the lives of everyday Catholics. These include diocesan-sponsored schools (often high schools), hospitals, and social-service agencies such as nursing homes or homes for unwed mothers. Besides supporting diocesan efforts, the Church in Rome undertakes some activities directly, for example, the support of missionaries. Catholics are asked, through special monthly collections, to support Church-sponsored causes outside the parish, such as the American Bishops' Overseas Appeal, Peter's Pence (the pope's discretionary spending fund), and the retirement fund for religious sisters. But few Catholics have direct knowledge of these programs or how the money is spent.

In recent years the Church has become more vocal in taking stands on controversial social issues. Pope John Paul II has been a frequent newsmaker through his many travels and his willingness to speak to local concerns during these visits. He has shown a willingness to provide a clear and unequivocal message not only on matters of faith and morals, but also on peace and justice issues through his encyclicals and other public pronouncements. Since the early 1980s, the U.S. Catholic Bishops have been at the forefront of the debate on U.S. policy

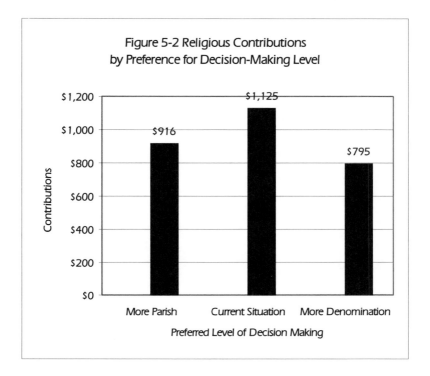

Figure 5-2 Religious Contributions
by Preference for Decision-Making Level

with their pastoral letters on peace (1983) and on economic justice (1985).

The point is that when Catholics are asked their opinion of the denominational-level activities of the Church, they are most likely thinking of diocesan-sponsored social-service programs, the support of foreign missions, or their view of the public pronouncements of the pope and bishops. They seldom have direct knowledge of the support functions played by the various denominational levels.

We asked our sample about how much enthusiasm they felt for the work and programs of the denomination. Nearly two-thirds (64%) gave the denominational programs either a very high or moderately high rating. This placed the Catholic Church's denominational approval rating slightly below that of the Assemblies of God (71%) and Southern Baptists (69%), but above that of Presbyterians (57%) and Lutherans (57%). This is noteworthy since, as described above, the Catholic Church is the most hierarchical of all the denominations in our sample. In fact, one of the distinguishing features of both the Assemblies of God and the Southern Baptists is their de-emphasis of any denominational hierarchy. When compared to Presbyterians and Lutherans, two churches where there is

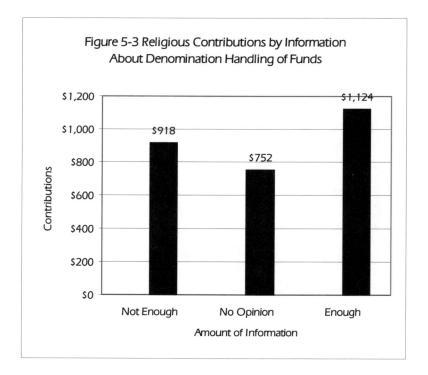

Figure 5-3 Religious Contributions by Information About Denomination Handling of Funds

some connection between the local church and the denomination, Catholics are much more satisfied with their denomination's programs.

As it turns out, satisfaction with the works and programs of the Catholic Church beyond the parish does influence giving. Figure 5-1 shows that Catholics who indicate enthusiasm for the larger Church's programs give more than those who don't. So Catholics aren't indifferent to the efforts of the Church beyond their parish, and whether or not they like the denomination's programs does play a role in their decision to contribute.

Denominational Decision-Making Processes

As we indicated in the opening chapter, some observers have blamed low Catholic giving on the laity's dissatisfaction with their level of participation in the Church's decision-making processes, both in general and in particular with respect to financial affairs. The decision-making issue can be considered from two perspectives: the denominational level and the parish level. Here we consider satisfaction with denominational-level decision-making and its effect on contributions. In the next chapter we assess the relationship between parish decision-making processes and giving. We asked our lay sample a series of related questions concerning lay input into denominational decision-making. First we asked about general decision-making processes. In our sample, fewer than half (49%) felt they had sufficient influence in the Church's decision-making. This was well below the figure for the other four denominations that we studied. In each of them, about two-thirds of the laity felt they had sufficient influence. But any concerns that the laity may feel with regards to their lack of influence was not evident in their decision to contribute to the Church. There was no significant difference between the household contributions of those who believed that they had enough influence and those who felt that they did not.

Next, we asked about the division of decision-making authority between the denomination and the parish. About one-third of our sample liked the current division of decision-making authority; 44% of our sample thought more decision making should be made at the local parish level; and about 4% wanted more decision making at the denominational level. The others had no opinion. This placed Catholics at about the midway point on this issue compared to the Protestants in our sample. A greater proportion of the Assemblies of God and Southern Baptists liked the current division in their denomination, while a smaller proportion of Presbyterians and Lutherans liked the current situation. All except the Assemblies of God would like more parish-level authority than the Catholics in our sample. Is this an important factor in influencing religious contributions? Yes. As Figure 5-2 indicates, those Catholics who are satisfied with the current division of decision-making authority contribute significantly more than those who prefer either more parish-level or more denominational-level authority.

What about decision-making specifically regarding church finances? Only about one-third of our Catholic sample thought they had enough information about the denomination's handling and allocation of funds. This is a very low figure. It compares with 46% for both the Lutherans and Presbyterians and slightly more than half of the Assemblies of God and Southern Baptists. But this is an important issue. Those who felt they did have enough information contributed significantly more than others (Figure 5-3).

We asked our sample if they trusted the denomination leaders' handling and allocation of funds. About 46% of the Catholics in the sample indicated a high level of trust. Another 45% demonstrated a medium level of trust. This was similar to the figure for the other denominations, except for the Assemblies of God, where more than two-thirds of the sample displayed a high degree of trust. But this turned out not to be an issue affecting religious contributions. Since so many people exhibited trust in their denominational leaders' handling of funds, giving was not significantly different for households with different degrees of trust.

On a related matter, we asked our sample if denominational leaders are sufficiently accountable to members regarding how church contributions are used. About 44% of the Catholics either strongly or moderately agreed that they were. This was the same percentage as Presbyterians, but well below the figures for the Assemblies of God (62%) and Southern Baptists (56%), and slightly lower than Lutherans (50%). But once again, it didn't seem to make much difference. Household contributions of those who gave the Church a high rating on accountability didn't differ significantly from those who gave it a low rating.

Finally, we asked two "bottom-line" questions about decision-making in the denomination. We asked if the leadership of the denomination was doing a good job. Almost three-fourths (71%) of our Catholic sample either strongly or moderately agreed that they were. This was below the approval rating for the Assemblies of God (82%), but well above that of the Presbyterians (54%), Lutherans (66%), and Southern Baptists (60%). Again, this is striking, given the very hierarchical nature of the Catholic Church. The leaders of the Church, most notably Pope John Paul II, but also including the local bishops, are evidently very popular and enjoy a great deal of support from the laity. Does this matter when it comes to giving to the Church? Yes. Figure 5-4 illustrates that those who agreed that the denominational leadership was doing a good job contributed significantly more than those who either disagreed or weren't sure.

The other "bottom-line" question concerned the decision-making processes in the denomination. A much smaller proportion of Catholics (54%) approved of their denomination's decision-making process than approved of their denominational leadership. The leaders are more popular than the processes that they oversee. This placed Catholics about in the middle of the approval rating for denominational decision-making processes. They were tied with the Lutherans (also 54%), ahead of the Presbyterians (49%), but trailing both the Assemblies of God (70%) and the Southern Baptists (62%). Again, the question is, does it matter in determining contributions? The answer is a qualified yes. Figure 5-5 shows that household contributions were slightly higher for those respondents who approved of the denomination's decision-making processes.

Denominational Financial Need

One of the theories attempting to explain low Catholic giving is that Catholics believe that the Church is wealthy, and really doesn't need

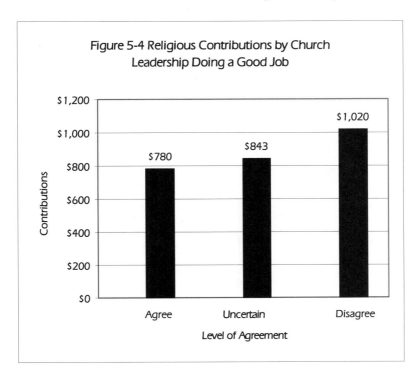

Figure 5-4 Religious Contributions by Church Leadership Doing a Good Job

Figure 5-5 Religious Contributions by Agreement With Denomination's Decision-Making Processes

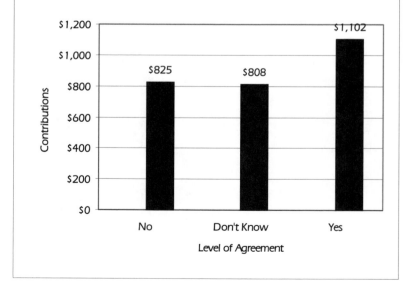

Figure 5-6 Religious Contributions by Denomination Has Serious Financial Needs

their contributions. We asked our sample if they thought the Church as a whole had serious financial needs. Slightly more than half said yes. This was a much larger percentage than any of the other denominations in our sample. About 44% of the Presbyterians, 42% of both the Lutherans and Southern Baptists, and 22% of the Assemblies of God felt that their denomination had serious financial needs. Does this affect Catholics' willingness to give? The answer is yes. Catholics who were convinced that the Church does have serious financial needs contributed significantly more than those who didn't believe it does or simply didn't know (Figure 5-6).

Conclusions

So what can we conclude about the relationship between Catholics' attitudes toward their denomination's programs and processes and their willingness to contribute to their churches? Do Catholics approve of how their denomination is run, and if so, does it affect their giving?

The Catholics in our sample gave generally high ratings to denominational-level programs (at least to the extent they understood them). Those who liked the denomination's programs contributed more.

With regards to Church processes, though, the evidence is mixed, and open to interpretation. On the one hand, Catholics (both on an absolute level and relative to the other denominations in our sample) felt they did not have sufficient influence in Church decision-making, lacked information on how Church funds were spent, and didn't think denominational leaders were accountable on how contributions were used. But for all three of these factors, there was either no significant impact on household contributions or those who were satisfied with the processes contributed more. One way to interpret this seeming contradiction is to conclude that Catholics really don't want any role in their Church's decision-making processes. Just because someone feels that they lack information on how funds are spent doesn't necessarily mean they think they should have that information. They might be just as happy not knowing. Perhaps they possess a strong belief in a hierarchical church and are willing to place unquestioning trust in their leadership.

The other interpretation is that many Catholics do want an input into the Church's decision-making processes. Their contributions are low because they feel shut out of some basic decisions, such as how their contributions are spent. According to this interpretation, if Church processes were more open, and the laity had more of a say, contributions would increase.

Both sides of this debate can find evidence in this chapter to support their interpretation. Those who support the current situation, with the laity receiving relatively little information and exerting little influence on Church decision-making, can point to the fact that the Catholic leadership received a very high rating, and a majority of the Catholics in our sample (54%) did approve of current denominational decision-making processes.

Those who believe Catholics should have more input into the Church's decision-making processes could point out that, in many instances, the Catholics in our sample gave their church the lowest approval on issues of openness of denominational decision-making processes, compared to the four Protestant denominations in the study. All four Protestant denominations receive significantly higher contributions from their members than does the Catholic Church. They could also point to the fact that more Catholics in our sample (44%) expressed a preference for more decision making at the parish level, as opposed to 33% who preferred the current division of decision-making authority.

The tension between the laity and the hierarchy over the amount of influence the laity should have is one that cuts across many dimensions of Church life, not just finances. D'Antonio et al. (1996) asked their sample of Catholics if the laity should have the right to participate in the decision-making for a broad range of issues. These included church finances, but also included selecting their parish priests and making policy about divorce, birth control, and women's ordination. For each of these, more than 60% of the respondents thought the laity should participate. We pick up on this issue in the next chapter when we examine the relationship between decision-making at the parish level and contributions.

References

D'Antonio, William V., James D. Davidson, Dean R. Hoge, and Ruth A. Wallace. *Laity: American and Catholic*. Kansas City: Sheed & Ward, 1996.

Kennedy, Eugene. *Tomorrow's Catholics, Yesterday's Church*. Liguori, MO: Triumph Books, 1995.

Vallet, Ronald E. and Charles E. Zech. *The Mainline Church's Funding Crisis: Issues and Possibilities*. Grand Rapids, MI: William B. Eerdmans, 1995.

6

Parish Programs
and Processes

The issues that have been covered so far in this book can be considered to some extent to be merely laying the groundwork. In many ways they can be likened to the preliminary fights at a boxing match. Some are more interesting than others, but most observers know that the real action will occur in the main event. When it comes to religious giving, the main event is at the parish level. Personal characteristics and beliefs, as we have seen, can play an important role. Most practicing Catholics cherish their denominational affiliation, and many are influenced by Church leadership, programs, and policies. But the parish is really where the Church has the greatest ability to impact individual religious giving.

This chapter considers a variety of parish-level characteristics that affect religious contributions. They are especially important because many of them (parish programs, quality of preaching and liturgies, decision-making processes, stewardship programs, etc.) could realistically undergo adjustments without affecting any of the basic underlying truths of the Catholic faith. Also, the Church (depending somewhat on the individual diocese) grants pastors a relatively large degree of autonomy (some are referred to as "the popes of their parish"). From a policy perspective, the topics discussed in this chapter offer many more opportunities for innovation than do those discussed elsewhere in this book. Most of those other topics are, for ecclesiastical and practical reasons, beyond the scope of anyone interested in making changes in order to increase Catholic giving. It's at the parish level that the greatest strides can be made to induce Catholics to increase their giving.

Parish Size

The belief that the large size of Catholic parishes inhibits giving has become virtually a universal truth. Nearly every researcher who has considered the relationship between parish size and contributions has concluded that large Catholic parishes are associated with low Catholic giving. In fact, some have concluded that it is the single biggest reason to explain low Catholic giving relative to that of Protestants (see Zaleski and Zech, 1994; Hoge and Augustyn, 1997).

Three reasons are generally cited for this finding. The first is that large parishes suffer from congestion. This decreases the quality of parish-level activities. In large parishes parishioners may be unable to make an appointment to meet with a priest on a timely basis. The reception of some sacraments might be less personalized. For example, there might be three or four children receiving the Sacrament of Baptism at a particular service, rather than just one; two or three weddings scheduled for a particular Saturday; or (this might be wishful thinking in this day and age) long lines to receive the Sacrament of Reconciliation. Congestion might also occur at non-sacramental parish activities, reducing some members' enjoyment and willingness to participate. Congestion means that not all parishioners can fit into the church at the same Mass, requiring multiple Sunday Masses. This diminishes the parish's ability to foster a sense of community. And, of course, getting out of the parking lot after Sunday Mass can be a near occasion of sin for many Catholics.

A second reason is that large parishes impede the development of a sense of ownership among the parishioners. Parishioners need to feel that the parish is "theirs" in order to fully support it. They need to believe that they have a say in matters such as liturgy, parish programs, budgets, etc. Protestants contribute more, it is argued, because their smaller congregations give each member a greater sense of ownership, and therefore a greater sense of urgency, over what happens in the congregation. In many denominations, this even extends to the right to select their own pastor.

Finally, large parishes are believed to hamper giving because they lead to a behavior called "free-riding." This occurs when parish members, seeing the large membership in their church, say to themselves, "Look at all the people who belong to this parish and support it. Surely no one will notice, and the church won't be affected, if I contribute less than I am able." Naturally, a few free-riders won't have much of an impact. But the larger the parish, the greater the tendency for many parishioners to become free-riders. This does not necessarily mean that they don't contribute at all (although parishes typically have a large number of households on their rolls who in fact don't contribute anything). Rather, free-ridership results in members contributing less than they could.

The myth that large parishes, because of congestion, the inability to develop a sense of ownership, and free-ridership, receive lower giving has been supported elsewhere. What did we find? We found that medium-sized parishes (1,001 to 2,500 members) receive significantly larger per-household contributions than do either smaller or larger parishes (Figure 6-1). Members of the very largest parishes (more than 5,000 members) were the next most generous. Households belonging to the smallest parishes (1,000 or fewer members) were among the lowest givers. Incidentally, this same trend prevailed when we compared giving with parish size as measured by the number of households. Again, medium-sized parishes received greater per-household contributions than either larger or smaller parishes, but those differences were not statistically significant.

This pattern has been found elsewhere. Jeff Rexhausen and Michael Cieslak (1994) studied giving among parishes in the Cincinnati archdiocese. They found that household contributions were greater in medium-sized parishes (membership of 1,001 to 2,000 in their sample) than in either larger or smaller parishes. In fact, household contributions in the smallest parishes were the lowest.

The myth that large Catholic parishes are a cause of low Catholic giving can only be partially supported. We certainly can't support the myth that they are the primary cause. There is an optimal parish size somewhere in the range of 1,000 to 2,500 members. Parishioners in larger parishes contribute less, but so do members of smaller parishes. Not much has been written about low giving in smaller parishes, because other studies have generally concluded that small parishes are good. They offer less congestion, more of a sense of ownership, and less free-riding. We can only speculate as to why giving would be low in small parishes. It might be because small parishes lack the resources to offer a broad range of programs. Perhaps opportunities for parish involvement are blocked by small groups and cliques. Maybe they are routinely assigned lower-quality priests. There are a multitude of explanations. But it is clear that, at least with regard to their ability to cultivate monetary contributions, small parishes are no better than large parishes. Why the discrepancy between these findings and those of the vast majority of other studies? One obvious reason is methodological. This study measured giving by surveying a random sample of parishioners and asking their

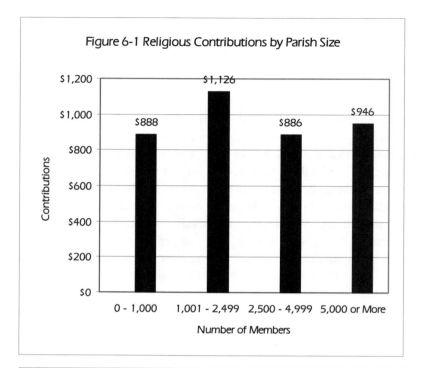

Figure 6-1 Religious Contributions by Parish Size

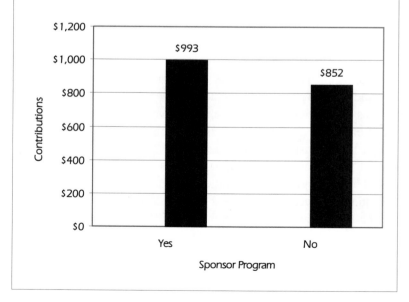

Figure 6-2 Religious Contributions by Sponsorship of Prayer or Study Group

actual household contributions. As stated earlier, this might have resulted in inflated estimates of per-household contributions. But it is doubtful that any bias was systematically related to parish size. Most other studies, in contrast, have calculated per-household contributions by simply taking total parish contributions and dividing them by the total number of parish households. This can lead to inaccuracies. Parishes differ widely in their willingness and ability to keep accurate statistics on the number of registered households. Some parishes keep close tabs on households joining and leaving the parish. Other parishes seldom "clean their rolls," and may continue to list deceased members or those who have moved away long after the event. Actually, the case could be made that larger parishes have the most difficulty keeping track of the comings and goings of their parishioners. As a result, the number of households registered in Catholic parishes is virtually a random variable, related to how recently they have cleaned their rolls. Any calculation based on that figure is subject to error. In fact, the American Congregational Giving Study collected data on both total parish contributions and the number of registered parish households. When we calculated per-household giving by merely dividing contributions by registered households and compared it to parish size, we also got the result that the larger the parish, the lower the giving. However, we rejected this approach (and its resulting outcome) because we didn't believe the denominator (registered households), and therefore the value of per-household contributions, was reliable.

Parish Programs and Activities

Parish Programs

It is part of the conventional wisdom that parish programs and services positively affect contributions. Parishioners respond to good programs in general. They especially respond when their parish offers a particular program where they have an interest, where they can find a niche. But this hypothesis has received little empirical support. This may be because of the difficulty in collecting data on the quantity and quality of programs. Some researchers have considered the impact of paid parish staff on contributions, but their findings were ambiguous (see Zaleski and Zech, 1994, and Cieslak, 1984).

We asked our sample about parish programs. First, we asked the parishes about the extent to which they offered 12 different programs, including various types of children's and adult education, prayer groups, men's groups, women's groups, seniors' groups, singles' groups, etc. Only one, the sponsorship of prayer or study groups at church, significantly

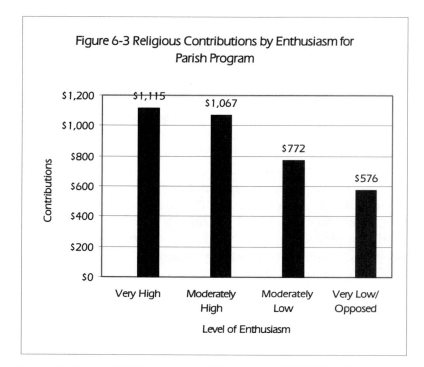

Figure 6-3 Religious Contributions by Enthusiasm for Parish Program

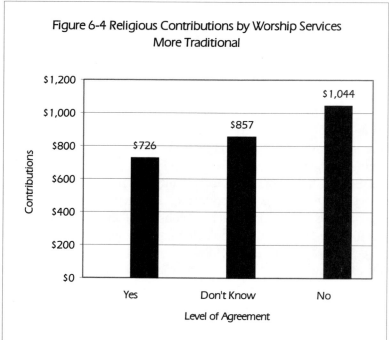

Figure 6-4 Religious Contributions by Worship Services More Traditional

affected contributions (Figure 6-2). We also asked about the total number of programs. We hypothesized that more programs would attract larger contributions, because they would increase the chances of someone finding a niche in the parish. But the number of programs was not significantly related to contributions.

We asked our sample about their general level of enthusiasm for their parish's programs. As Figure 6-3 demonstrates, people who were the most enthusiastic about the work of their parish contributed significantly more than those who lacked enthusiasm. So, while we were unable to specify which programs, or even the number of programs, that induce parishioners to contribute, we can confirm the conventional wisdom that parishioners who like their parish's programs do contribute more.

Liturgy

There are other aspects of parish life that, while they're not exactly programs, fall into the same general category. One of these is liturgy. It's been more than 30 years since Vatican II completely revamped the Catholic Mass. It's changed from a passive, non-participatory gathering performed in a foreign tongue to a more active, participatory assembly rendered in the vernacular. Still today, parishioners can be found who long for the pre-Vatican II Masses that they cherished. They resent the appearance of guitars and popular music at Mass, and yearn for the days of Latin Masses, Gregorian chant, and incense. Others feel the Church hasn't changed its liturgies enough. They want an even more festive atmosphere, with a broader range of music and more lay participation. So naturally the question arises, are contributions affected by the traits of a parish's liturgies? The answer is no. We asked our sample two related questions. One, aimed at those who yearn for "the good old days," asked if they'd contribute more if their parish's worship services were more traditional. Two-thirds said no. As Figure 6-4 shows, those who told us no gave significantly more. Does this mean that parishes should speed up their implementation of new, innovative liturgies? No. We also asked our sample if they would give more if their parish's worship services were more modern. Almost three-fourths (72%) indicated they wouldn't. Figure 6-5 reveals that those who said no to more modern liturgies also gave more.

What can we conclude from the seemingly contradictory responses to this pair of questions? Catholics like their current liturgies. They don't want to go back to the old days of "bells and smells" Masses. Nor do they want different, trendy activities at their Masses. Parishes that can

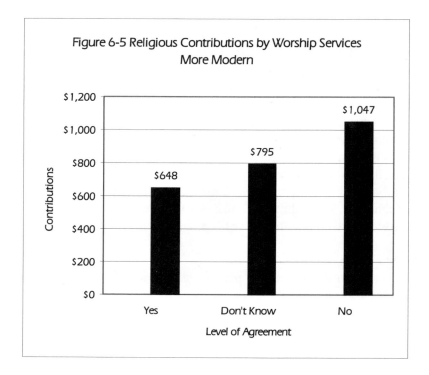

Figure 6-5 Religious Contributions by Worship Services More Modern

navigate a middle course between these two extremes will attract larger contributions.

Preaching

It is also widely accepted that religious contributions are related to the quality of the homilies that are preached each week. As with other goods and services, both secular and religious, quality is in the eyes of the beholder. For some, a quality homily is one that plays on some varia- tion of a fire-and-brimstone theme. Others prefer homilies that speak to the struggles that they encounter as Christians trying to cope in a gener- ally immoral or amoral society. In either case, one would expect those who are more satisfied with the preaching that they receive are also more generous when it comes to giving to the Church.

We asked our sample if they would contribute more if the preaching in their parish was more meaningful (however they defined it). Most (60%) said they wouldn't. Those who told us no contributed signifi- cantly more than those who said yes, or weren't sure (Figure 6-6). Does this mean that Catholics don't want better homilies? Or that, contrary to what most believe, the quality of homilies doesn't affect religious contributions? Probably not, although we didn't specifically ask either of those questions. Rather, it probably indicates that they're pretty well satisfied with the homilies that they're currently receiving, and this is already reflected in their giving. Better homilies wouldn't have much of an additional impact on their decision to give.

Parish Message

Over time, a parish can develop the reputation for emphasizing a specific message. For example, some parishes become known for their outreach to the larger community. Others might be celebrated for their commitment to Catholic education. Still others might be renowned for their spirituality. In many cases, these had been the priority of long-term influential pastors. Parishioners came to identify with them and continued them even after the pastor had left.

We asked our sample about two possible themes. First, we asked if they would contribute more if they found the parish to be more spiritually nourishing. More than half (54%) indicated no. Those who said no contributed significantly more than others (Figure 6-7). Are we to conclude that parishioners don't want more spiritual nourishment? Of course

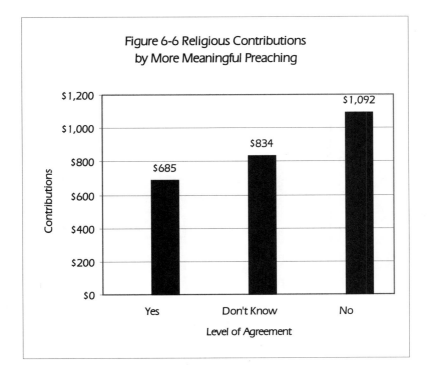

Figure 6-6 Religious Contributions by More Meaningful Preaching

not. We can probably interpret this response as similar to the response on preaching. Parishioners probably find their parishes to be spiritually nourishing, and have already factored that into their contributions.

The second theme we asked about was the parish's attention to social issues. We asked about the parish paying both more attention to social issues and less attention to social issues. This was to recognize that some Catholics are more other-worldly, while others think the Church should be more concerned with the social ills of this world. The results were similar to the pair of questions that we asked about worship services. A majority of parishioners indicated that they would not give more if the parish paid more attention to social issues (57%). They contributed significantly more than those who said they would, or who didn't know (Figure 6-8). But a substantial majority (70%) told us they wouldn't give more if the parish paid less attention to social issues. They, too, contributed more than those who indicated either that they would give more, or they didn't know, although the differences, while large, were not statistically significant. Again, these results can be interpreted like those of the relationship between satisfaction with liturgies and giving. Parishioners are satisfied with the

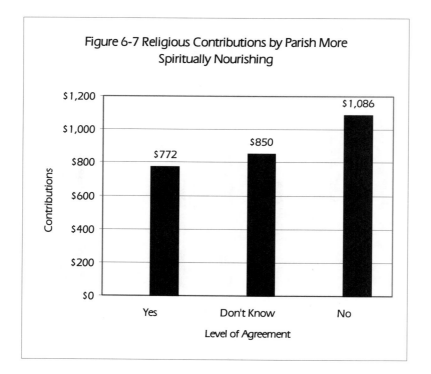

Figure 6-7 Religious Contributions by Parish More Spiritually Nourishing

level of social action in their parishes. They have already factored that satisfaction into their decision to contribute.

Parish Decision-Making Processes

Mirroring their hierarchical denominational structure, Catholic parishes have also had a history of top-down management. Whatever "Father said" became unquestioning parish policy, often simply because "Father said." It didn't seem to matter whether the issue concerned faith and morals, liturgies, parish spending, or even which political candidates to endorse. Much of that has changed since Vatican II. Catholics now recognize that, through baptism, they not only have a right but an obligation to participate in parish decision-making. The Church is not a democracy, but the expectation is that parishioners will accept responsibility for the life of the parish through their participation on parish councils, finance committees, liturgy committees, and so on.

Much has changed in the realm of parish decision-making since Vatican II, but not everything. Some pastors still view themselves as the sole decision-maker in the parish, and resent "lay intrusion." Many parishio-

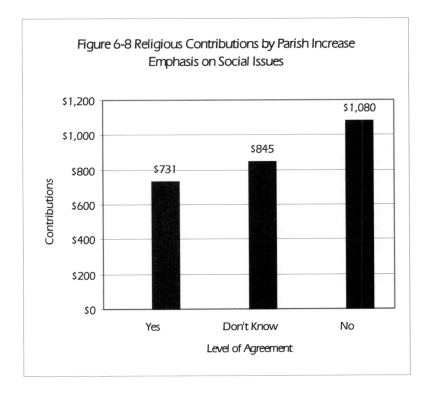

Figure 6-8 Religious Contributions by Parish Increase Emphasis on Social Issues

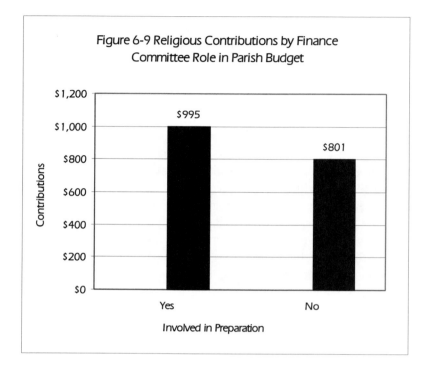

Figure 6-9 Religious Contributions by Finance Committee Role in Parish Budget

ners feel comfortable with the priest making all of their parish's decisions for them. Just because a parish claims on paper to have a parish council or a finance committee doesn't necessarily mean that shared decision-making is occurring.

In the previous chapter we found that Catholics rate their input into denominational decision-making much lower than did the other denominations in our sample. But we also found that those who were satisfied with their role were more generous contributors. This combination could be used to support either of two radically different interpretations of the relationship between lay input into denominational decision-making processes and contributions. Are the same sort of relationships found at the parish level?

Parish Budgetary Processes

Our first interest is with preparing the parish budget. This is perhaps the most critical area for lay input. Budgetary decisions on how parish funds are spent set the tone for the parish and determine its priorities. Will the school get more money? What about the CCD program? Should we increase our support for CYO activities? How much should we allo-

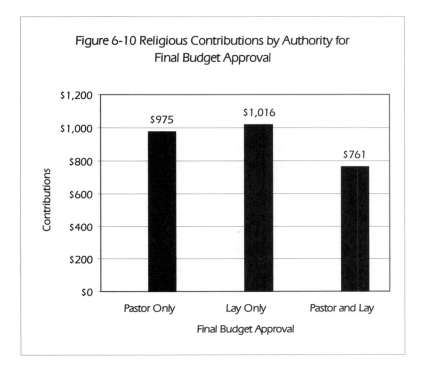

Figure 6-10 Religious Contributions by Authority for Final Budget Approval

cate for outreach efforts to the less-fortunate members of our community? In parish life, as in government, "He who controls the purse strings controls the kingdom."

There are two separate but related aspects here: preparing the budget, and approving the budget. It's difficult to say which is more important. While final approval implies the ability to make last-minute changes, in many cases these changes are marginal. And while those preparing the budget have the ability to set the agenda for the entire parish, their power is limited if their spending allocations can be overturned at the time of final approval.

We asked our sample of parishes about who had input into the preparation of the budget, and who had the final approval of the budget. The pastor was involved in the preparation of the budget in almost all of the parishes in our sample (94%). The parish-finance committee typically also had some input (83%). The paid staff participated in the preparation of the budget in only about half (52%) of the parishes. In only about a third of the parishes (34%) was the parish council involved. The rest of the parishioners assisted in the preparation of the budget in fewer than 10% of the parishes.

Who had the final approval? The pastor alone had the final approval of the budget in more than two-thirds (69%) of the parishes. In another 2% of the parishes the pastor shared final authority with the finance committee, and in 6% of the parishes the pastor, finance committee, and parish council jointly exercised final budgetary approval. The finance committee alone had the final say in 11% of the parishes. The parish council had that responsibility in 8% of the parishes. None of the parishes in our sample gave final approval to the parishioners as a group.

Does any of this make a difference in parishioners' contributions? Only in two cases. Parishes where the finance committee had input into developing the budget received significantly higher contributions than those where that committee was not involved (Figure 6-9). It didn't matter one way or another if the pastor, parish council, staff, or general parish were part of the process.

Second, parishes where the pastor was not involved in the final approval of the budget received higher per-household contributions than in those parishes where he assumed some responsibility, either by himself or in conjunction with other parish organizations (Figure 6-10).

Attacking the issue from another perspective, we asked parishioners

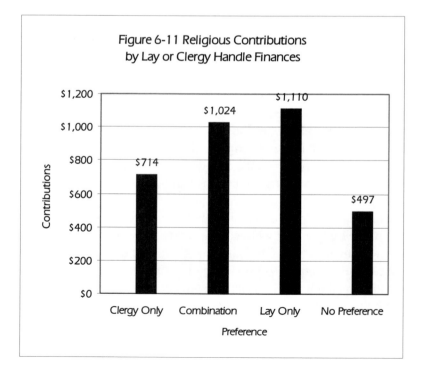

if they preferred that priests or the laity handle parish financial matters. More than three-fourths (78%) responded that they favored a combination of priests and lay members. Those who supported a combination gave slightly less than those who preferred lay only. Both groups contributed significantly more than those who thought that priests alone should control parish finances (Figure 6-11).

Do parishioners think that they have enough information about the handling of funds in their parish? Since they are not a part of the budgetary process in most parishes, it's not surprising that only slightly more than half (53%) thought they did. This is well below the figure for the Protestants in our sample. In every other denomination in our sample, at least 70% (and in the case of Southern Baptists, more than 80%) of the respondents felt they had enough information concerning the handling of parish funds. Giving was significantly higher in those parishes where the laity believe that they had sufficient information about how parish funds were spent (Figure 6-12).

But maybe Catholics are satisfied with their lack of information concerning parish financial matters. Maybe they're happy to have the parish budget dictated to them. Perhaps they don't want any input into parish

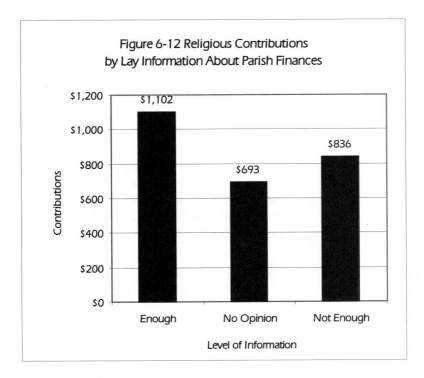

Figure 6-12 Religious Contributions by Lay Information About Parish Finances

financial decision-making. We asked our sample if they thought parishioners had enough influence in parish financial decision-making. Fewer than half (48%) thought that they did. Again, this was considerably below the figure for the Protestants in our sample. More than two-thirds of the members of each of the other denominations (and more than three-fourths of the Southern Baptists) agreed that typical members had adequate influence in congregational financial issues. Possessing this influence made a difference in Catholic giving. Figure 6-13 shows us that those Catholics who believed that they had ample influence contributed more.

It appears that Catholics, at least relative to Protestants, wish that laypeople had more say in parish financial matters. But given that they lack that input, are they satisfied with the parish budget that does emerge? We asked them if they thought their parish's budget priorities were acceptable. Barely more than half (53%) either strongly or moderately agreed that their parish's budget priorities were appropriate. This lagged behind the approval figures for the other denominations, which ranged from 69% (Lutherans) to 80% (Southern Baptists). And, once again, we find this to be a significant factor in determining Catholic contributions (Figure 6-14).

Finally, we asked about two important and somewhat related issues: the accountability and trustworthiness of the parish leadership in financial matters. Most Catholics found their leadership accountable, with 61% of our sample agreeing either strongly or moderately that parish leaders were accountable regarding the use of their contributions. But the corresponding figure was more than 70% for each of the four Protestant denominations in the sample. Catholics who found their parish leadership to be accountable contributed significantly more (Figure 6-15).

It should go without saying that trustworthiness is a critical element across the board in the relationship between a pastor and his parishioners. This is especially true when it comes to money. Anyone who hopes to induce voluntary contributions from a group must, at a minimum, have the trust of that group. Parishioners have a natural inclination to want to trust their pastor. Most feel that if they can't trust their pastor with their contributions, whom can they trust? The vast majority of priests are holy and spiritual men and eminently deserving of that trust. Therefore, it's not surprising that nearly two-thirds of the Catholic parishioners in our sample indicated that they placed a high level of trust in the parish leadership (which would primarily be the pastor) when it came to the handling of their funds. Unfortunately, this is the lowest of any of the

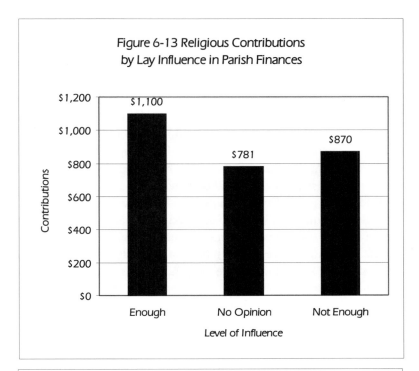

Figure 6-13 Religious Contributions
by Lay Influence in Parish Finances

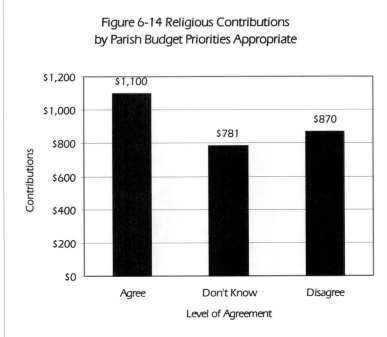

Figure 6-14 Religious Contributions
by Parish Budget Priorities Appropriate

denominations in our sample. More than 80% of the Assemblies of God and Southern Baptists placed a high degree of trust in their congregational leadership. Is this because Catholic pastors are less worthy of this trust? No. The answer probably lies in the failure of Catholic pastors to provide information and accountability on parish financial matters. Throughout this section, we've seen that Catholics believe they have less information and that their leadership is less accountable to them than in Protestant congregations. All of this combined has resulted in lower levels of trust in their parish leadership. Does this affect contributions? Figure 6-16 shows that Catholics who had a high degree of trust in their leadership's ability to handle parish finances contributed more.

We asked the question in a myriad of ways, and each time we received the same answer: Catholic parishioners want more lay input into the financial decision-making process in their parish. They want the laity involved in both constructing and approving the budget. They want budget information disseminated. They want their pastors to be accountable to them as to how their parish spends its money. Parishioners who believe the budget process is open, who believe the typical layperson has some meaningful input into the parish financial decision-making process, will contribute more.

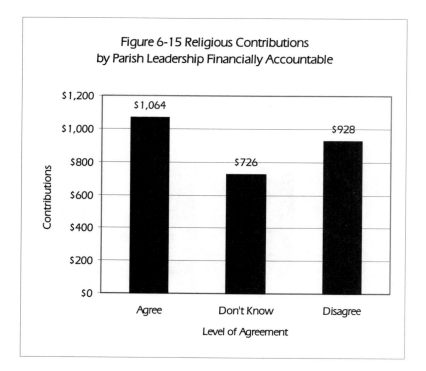

Figure 6-15 Religious Contributions by Parish Leadership Financially Accountable

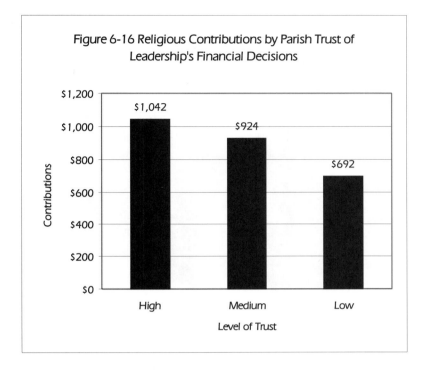

Figure 6-16 Religious Contributions by Parish Trust of Leadership's Financial Decisions

Other Parish Decision-Making

The Catholics in our sample sent us a clear message concerning their desire to be involved in their parish's decision-making process when money is involved. What about other parish activities? Do parishioners want the same level of input in other parish matters such as liturgy, evangelization, religious education, etc.? Generally speaking, the answer is yes. For example, we asked our sample if opportunities to serve in parish leadership roles were generally available. Some parishes are notorious for the fact that the pastor alone controls appointment to the key parish committees and their chairs. In other parishes, a small clique of laypeople might exert undue influence over parish committee appointments. Slightly more than 85% of the Catholics in our sample agreed that parish leadership opportunities were generally available. While lower than the corresponding value for the Protestant denominations, it is still a very healthy level. Their contributions were significantly larger (Figure 6-17) than those who felt blocked from holding leadership positions.

We also asked about the extent to which important parish decisions are made after an open discussion between the parish leadership and the members. Only 47% of our Catholic sample either strongly or moder-

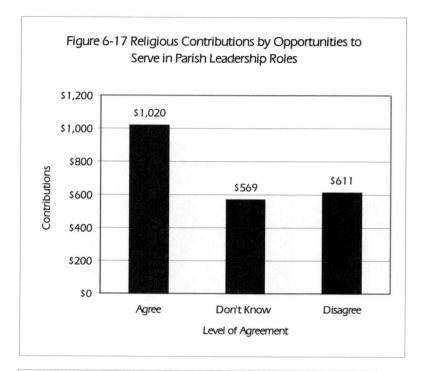

Figure 6-17 Religious Contributions by Opportunities to Serve in Parish Leadership Roles

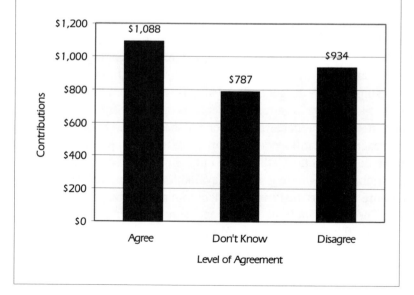

Figure 6-18 Religious Contributions by Leadership Discusses Important Parish Decisions

ately agreed that these discussions took place in their parish. In each of the Protestant denominations, nearly three-fourths of the respondents agreed that these discussions occurred. Figure 6-18 demonstrates that Catholics in those parishes where open discussions took place contributed at significantly higher levels.

Finally, we asked our sample if they approved of the overall decision-making process in their parish. While 72% expressed their approval, more than 80% of each of the Protestant denominations in our sample approved of their congregation's overall decision-making process. Catholics who approved of their parish's overall decision-making process contributed more, but the differences were not statistically significant.

From this we can conclude that lay Catholics respond favorably when they are given an input into overall parish decision-making, not just in the financial area. This positive reaction translates into larger contributions.

Parish School

Whether or not parish schools foster larger contributions from the parishioners is open to debate. We had some parishioners tell us about how critical the parochial school was to the life of the parish, how the school produces commitment to the parish, and how all parish activities centered around the life of the school. Other parishioners described their parochial school as a large vacuum cleaner that sucked up parish resources. They claimed that a large portion of the parish budget went toward the support of a program (the school) that served a small minority of the parishioners. This debate can become especially animated in suburban parishes, where many parishioners are paying high taxes to support their public-school system and resent their religious contributions being used to support an (in their opinion) inferior educational alternative. This is also a controversial issue in some inner-city parishes, where a large percentage of the parochial-school students are not Catholic, but are enrolled in the parish school to avoid substandard public schools.

A total of 69% of the parishes in our sample supported a parochial school, either by themselves (39%) or in conjunction with other parishes in a consolidated school (30%). The average annual cost incurred by those parishes that supported a school by themselves was $406,500. Most of this cost was covered by tuition revenue. The average was $225,900 (56% of total costs). Direct parish subsidies covered another $138,700 (34%). The remainder came from fund-raising (7%) and other sources, including indirect subsidies (for example, sharing utility costs and janitorial services with the rest of the parish). Naturally, the costs for those parishes that co-sponsored a consolidated parochial school were much lower — about $98,000 per parish in direct and indirect subsidies. The school subsidy in those parishes that had their own parochial school averaged about 27% of the parish budget. In those parishes with consolidated schools, the average subsidy was 20% of the parish budget.

What have other studies learned about the effect of parochial schools on parishioners' giving? Surprisingly little. In fact, most researchers didn't even examine the relationship between the existence of a school and contributions. Michael Welch (1993) is one who did. He expected that the existence of a school would positively impact both his measures of parishioners' religious participation (monetary contributions and parish activity involvement) and devotion (worship attendance and participation in religious rituals). But it had no meaningful affect on any of them except for a modest impact on their giving.

Jeff Rexhausen and Michael Cieslak (1994) also considered the effect of schools on giving. Using data from the Cincinnati archdiocese, they found that diocese-wide, there was a slight relationship between giving and the existence of a school in the parish. But they received some stronger results when they broke their sample down geographically. The existence of a school had no effect on giving in large city or suburban parishes. But it had a strong and positive effect on giving in small city and rural parishes. In fact, the existence of a school was the single most important determinant of giving in small-city parishes.

Dean Hoge and Boguslaw Augustyn (1997) considered the effect of parish schools on giving in their nationwide sample of 1,682 parishes. They found that the existence of a school in a parish was associated with higher per-household giving (p. 56). The existence of a school had its greatest impact on giving in small (500 or fewer households) and medium-sized (501 to 1,500 households) parishes, but a smaller effect on giving in large (over 1,500 households) parishes.

The other prominent researcher to investigate the relationship between parochial schools and giving was Greeley (1987). Remember, Bishop McManus had hypothesized that low Catholic giving could be attributed to the fact that Catholics were burdened by paying high parochial-school tuition. This, the bishop thought, was in lieu of larger contributions to their parish. Greeley's data contradicted that viewpoint. He found that households with children in Catholic schools contributed more (even after having paid tuition) than those without children in parochial schools.

He even argued that their extra contributions were more than enough to pay the parish's subsidy, and that "Catholic schools not only supported themselves from higher Sunday contributions but indeed were a profitable enterprise for the Church" (p. 47).

There are really two related issues here. One concerns the contributions of those families who send their children to parochial schools. Do they contribute more, even after having made their tuition payments, than do other households? The other issue concerns the reaction of the entire parish to the school. Are parochial schools considered to be so essential in creating a sense of excitement and dynamism in a parish, are they so instrumental in enhancing not only the social life, but also the spiritual life of the parish, that their very existence results in larger parishioner contributions? Or are they a massive drain on the parish's resources that causes resentment and thus lower contributions among the other parishioners?

We should emphasize that when we asked parishioners about the amount that they gave, we specifically asked that they not include any tuition payments. On the other hand, we know of some parishes in which the school tuition is kept artificially low, but parents are required to meet

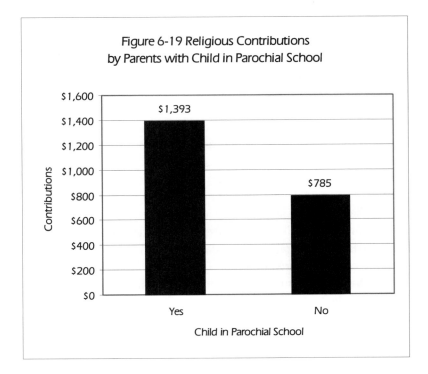

Figure 6-19 Religious Contributions by Parents with Child in Parochial School

a certain standard in their regular giving. This is done to give parents a tax break. School tuition is not tax-deductible, but religious contributions are. This practice inflates the amount of contributions made by households with parochial school children. It is illegal, but it is done. We have no way of knowing the extent to which, if any, this tactic may have affected our results.

Figure 6-19 shows the answer to the first question. Households that send their children to parochial schools do contribute significantly more than do other households. The data doesn't allow us to say with any certainty that this difference in annual contributions (about $600 per household) is sufficient to cover the parish subsidy. So this result alone doesn't allow us to support Greeley's claim that parochial schools are a profit center for parishes. But they certainly are consistent with his findings.

Is there support for Catholic schools as a boon to parish contributions, rather than a source of resentment, when we look at the larger picture? Do parishes that sponsor parochial schools receive larger contributions? A qualified yes. As Figure 6-20 illustrates, parishes that operated their own parochial school received significantly greater contributions per household than did other parishes. Surprisingly, parishes that didn't offer a school received higher contributions than parishes that co-sponsored a consolidated parochial school with other parishes. As an aside, we wondered if the effect of the parochial school on giving was related to how much parishioners were being asked to subsidize the school. So we looked at the relationship between the subsidy burden, as measured by the percent of total parish revenue that was used to subsidize the parish school, and household contributions. There was no significant relationship. Parishioners' contributions are not related to the amount of burden that the parish might feel in supporting the school.

What can we make of this pattern? One conclusion is that parents who send their children to parochial schools are among the most committed in the parish, at least as measured by their giving. Whether this commitment to the parish is a consequence of the impact of the school on their social or spiritual lives, we can't be certain. In fact it could well be that the causality runs the other way. Maybe it's the case that those Catholics who are the most committed to the Church in the first place tend to send their children to parochial schools. Whatever the cause, Catholics who send their children to parochial schools are more generous in their contributions.

Not only that, but commitment and generosity spill over to the rest of the parish. The higher per-household contributions of parishes that sponsor their own school provides at least tacit support for the theory that many parishioners consider the parish school to be a source of enrichment for the parish at large. But this support doesn't extend to consolidated schools. Not only do parishes that co-sponsor a school receive lower contributions than parishes with their own schools; they receive less than parishes without any school at all. Clearly, the value to the parish of a parochial school is not restricted to just the education it provides. Its impact on the everyday lives of the parish is also profound. But when the parishioners are not in direct (perhaps physical) contact with the school, these benefits are lost. Without the witness that the school provides, parishioners may come to resent the fact that their contributions are being used to support this "distant" project, just as they might resent their religious contributions being used to pay for a private academy. The consolidated school could be considered distant even if it happens to be physically located on parish grounds. The fact that it is shared with other parishes means that parishioners have lost their sense of involvement and ownership in the school. Just as "it takes a village to raise a child," it takes a parish. When that responsibility is shared with house-

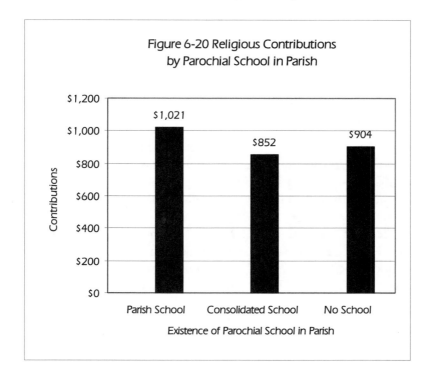

Figure 6-20 Religious Contributions by Parochial School in Parish

holds from other parishes, some of the commitment is lost. That seems to be the task that parishes that co-sponsor a consolidated parish face. How to reconcile the fact that parish schools are expensive, and require a large amount of resources, which the parish may not be able to afford on their own, with the need for the parish as a whole to feel a sense of involvement, even a sense of ownership, with the school? This is not an insurmountable task, but its critical nature must be recognized.

The fact that parishes with consolidated schools receive such low contributions shouldn't diminish the finding that parishes with their own parochial schools receive substantially larger contributions, both from families with children in the school and from other parishioners. In fact, it reinforces that finding. Greeley was right. Parochial schools seemingly do pay for themselves. Parishes considering merging their parochial school with nearby parishes should pay close attention to this fact.

Stewardship

Stewardship. The giving of our time, talent, and treasure to our church in recognition that all we have is really a gift from God. This is one of the trendiest topics in Catholic parishes today. The Bible contains numerous allusions to positive rewards for good stewardship. Protestants have been emphasizing it for years, our parishioners are being told. It's time we Catholics caught up.

Unfortunately, to many pastors, stewardship and money are synonymous. Too often stewardship is viewed as simply another fund-raising technique. How often have you heard pastors say something like, "I know that contributions of time and talent are probably important too, but right now our real need in this parish is financial. So let's emphasize the money aspects of stewardship for now. We'll get to the time and talent part as soon as we're financially stable." Not only is this bad theology, it's bad fund-raising. Appealing to the biblical precept of stewardship just to place another twist on a fund-raising campaign runs the risk of alienating parishioners.

In Chapter One we noted that the U.S. bishops had received a considerable amount of criticism over their refusal to include some practical recommendations in their 1992 pastoral on stewardship. Perhaps anticipating that criticism, the bishops had included a disclaimer in the introduction:

"Concentrating on one specific obligation of stewardship, even one as important as church support, could make it harder — even impossible — for people to grasp the vision. It could imply that when Bishops get serious about stewardship, what they really mean is simply giving money" (NCCB, 1992, p. 5).

This is a legitimate concern. There are a number of formalized "Stewardship Programs" available for parishes to adopt. Most place their primary focus on the money portion of stewardship, giving only lip service to the time and talent components. For example, one of the most popular is "Sacrificial Giving." It consists of five elements:

1. Giving Is Planned. It is part of a household's total financial plan that includes an intentional response to God's generosity.

2. Giving Is Proportionate. While the tithe is the biblical standard, parishioners not prepared to be tithers are nevertheless encouraged to think in terms of contributing a percentage of their income.

3. Giving Is Sacrificial. It should come from a household's substance, rather than it's abundance.

4. Giving Is Free. The giver places no conditions on the gift.

5. Giving Is a Prayer of Thanksgiving. It is most appropriately presented at the Offertory of the Mass (Harris, 1994, p. 230).

You don't have to read too carefully to observe that there is no mention of time and talent. We've seen sacrificial-giving literature that does mention time and talent, but it is always done as an afterthought.

We don't mean to imply that all stewardship programs only emphasize the money component, or that all pastors view stewardship as a fund-raising gimmick. We're only pointing out that the potential exists.

Besides focusing primarily on the financial impact of stewardship, there are other potential pitfalls that parishes considering introducing a stewardship program must avoid. Some of these revolve around the way the stewardship message is framed. Stewardship is not about something we do; it's about who we are, and whose we are. Through our faith in Jesus Christ, we are children of God and joint heirs with Christ (see Romans 8:17). Nor is stewardship about merely meeting the parish budget; it's about examining our attitude toward and our use of money. Stewardship is not just about good intentions and kind deeds; it's about recognizing that all life depends on God. Finally, it's not just an annual campaign designed to induce people to contribute to the church as yet another charity; it's about transformed visions, changed attitudes, and altered lives.

So how prevalent is stewardship in our sample of Catholic parishes? Sixteen percent of the parishes claimed to emphasize stewardship year-round. Another 44% emphasized it occasionally. This compares to the nearly 90% of the Protestant congregations in our sample who claimed

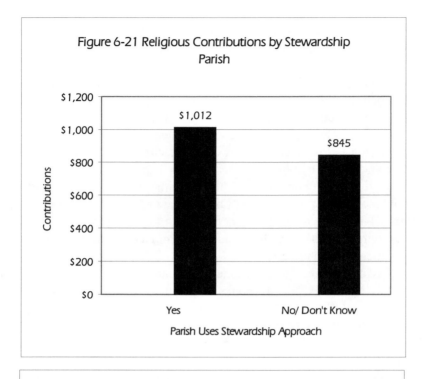

Figure 6-21 Religious Contributions by Stewardship Parish

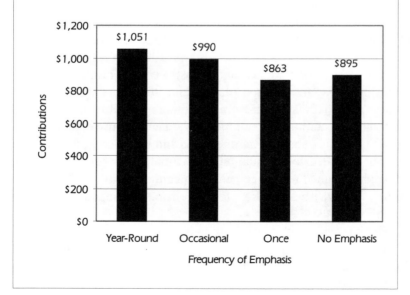

Figure 6-22 Religious Contributions by Frequency of Stewardship Message

to emphasize stewardship occasionally or year-round. Does emphasizing stewardship make a difference? Yes. We asked our sample if their parish promoted stewardship and whether or not it affected their giving. As Figure 6-21 illustrates, parishioners who belonged to stewardship parishes contributed significantly more than those who didn't or weren't sure. How often does the stewardship message need to be heard? Figure 6-22 shows us that household contributions increased with more regular stewardship emphasis.

Pledging

What about the various tactics associated with successful stewardship programs? For example, how about the practice of filling out annual pledge cards? We heard a lot of resistance from parishioners when this topic was raised in our focus-group interviews. Those who opposed it didn't like the idea of giving as an obligation. Some told us that if their parish relied on pledging, it would actually receive less money. People's pledges would be lower than they're currently giving. They'd be afraid to pledge as much as they currently give because some unknown might occur that might prevent them from meeting their pledge. They were unconvinced when we tried to point out the inconsistency in their argument. Some of the same people who were violently opposed to an annual pledge to support their church wouldn't hesitate to commit themselves to a four-year car loan. Others reacted negatively to the thought of pledging to support current church operations, but gladly made two-or-three year pledges to fund a capital campaign.

We should note that many Protestants were also opposed to pledging, and gave us the same reasoning as our Catholic focus groups. In fact, while 48% of the Catholics approved of the use of pledge cards, only 37% of the Assemblies of God and only 41% of the Southern Baptists did. Of course, these denominations teach that it is a Christian's duty to tithe. Pledging received a high approval rating among the Presbyterian sample (78%), but only moderate approval (58%) among Lutherans.

Does pledging among Catholics make a difference? Yes. Figure 6-23 shows that Catholics who approved of the practice of pledging contributed significantly more than others. In Figure 6-24, we see that those who actually filled out a pledge card gave at significantly higher levels.

A related issue concerns the extent to which Catholics plan their giving. Possibilities range from those Catholics who tithe to those who decide on Sunday morning how much they can afford to throw into the offertory basket that week. We'd expect that the more planning that goes into the religious-giving decision the greater the level of contributions. This would be true even for those who aren't officially pledging. Figure 6-25 confirms this suspicion. Those who tithed, of course, contributed the most. But those who had planned their giving for the year, either as a percentage of income or as an annual dollar-amount, contributed more than those whose giving is based on a weekly decision. The more effective that parishes are in convincing their people to determine their giving on an annual basis, whether through formal pledges or informal commitments, the larger will be their contributions.

Other Stewardship Tactics

There are other practices that parishes could employ as part of their stewardship campaign. For example, priests could preach sermons on the topic of stewardship. Laypeople might be invited to give testimonials at Mass about what their stewardship commitment has meant in their lives. The parish could disseminate promotional materials, such as brochures. These could be either distributed at Mass or mailed to every parish household. The stewardship committee could make an effort to telephone or even personally visit parishioners to talk about stewardship

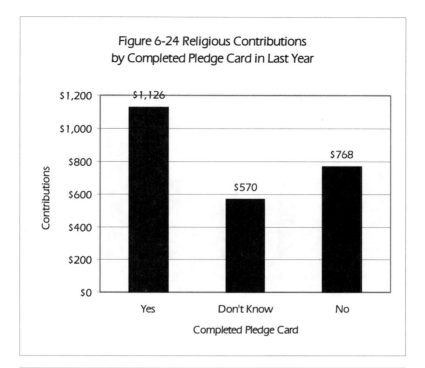

Figure 6-24 Religious Contributions by Completed Pledge Card in Last Year

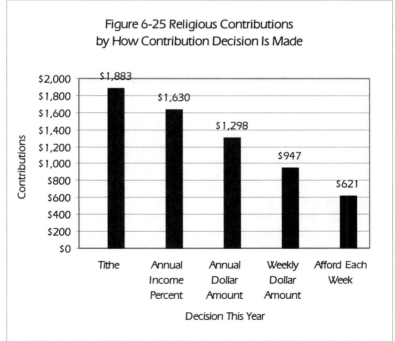

Figure 6-25 Religious Contributions by How Contribution Decision Is Made

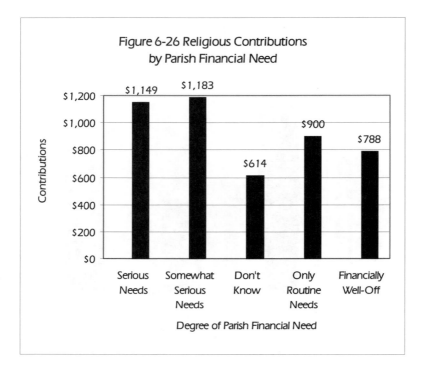

Figure 6-26 Religious Contributions
by Parish Financial Need

with them. We asked our sample about each of these practices. None of them was significantly related to giving.

It is clear, then, that lay Catholics are responsive to the stewardship message. Adopting a stewardship approach is not only sound theologically, but it will also make a parish better off financially. While there is some resistance to the concept of pledging (or filling out "commitment cards") among lay Catholics, parishioners who do pledge contribute more. But other stewardship techniques were unsuccessful in raising the level of contributions.

Parish Financial Need

Perhaps the antithesis of stewardship is an appeal for funds based on parish needs. This is a frequent tactic used by fund-raisers. They try to convince the donor that their cause is in serious financial straits. They appeal to the donor's sense of responsibility to make sure that this worthwhile endeavor is financially solvent. Donors respond out of a feeling of obligation or guilt.

We saw in Chapter Four that Catholics were more concerned than the others in our sample about their denomination's financial condition. Those who thought the Church had serious financial needs contributed more. At the parish level, just under 40% of our sample of Catholic parishioners thought that their parish had either serious or very serious financial needs. This was similar to the figure in our other four denominations. Is the message of parish financial need effective in increasing contributions? Yes. Parishioners who felt that their parish had some financial need contributed more than others (Figure 6-26). Appealing to the parishioners on the basis of parish financial need is not a stewardship message. But it can be effective if the parish's goal is to increase contributions.

Parish Teachings

Another one of the possible determinants of religious giving that has received little or no attention is the effect of individual parish teachings. The Catholic Faith discourages variance from official Church dogma. Furthermore, no one would suggest that a parish should compromise Church doctrine merely to increase giving. But individual parishes have been known to place different emphases on some Church precepts. For example, in Chapter Four we saw that when we asked our sample what the primary duty of Christians was, different responses were associated with different contribution levels. Of the four options that were provided, those who believed that their primary duty was to participate in Church traditions and sacraments were the highest givers. They were followed closely by those who believed that their primary duty was to change unjust social structures. To understand that issue from another angle, we asked the pastors in our sample which of the four possible messages did they emphasize in their parish. A large majority, 62%, said that of the alternatives provided, their primary emphasis was on following the teachings of Jesus as a basis for spiritual growth and fulfillment. Another 30% emphasized faithfully participating in the tradition and sacraments of the Church. This was no surprise, since the Catholic Church is very sacramental, and its teachings have historically relied on tradition. Only 5% indicated that their parish primarily emphasized helping others commit their lives to Christ, which is the response that we would have expected from some of the more conservative, evangelical Christians. Just 3% chose the more liberal response by indicating that their parish was primarily concerned with helping to change unjust or oppressive social structures. All are legitimate emphases and all are consistent with Catholic Church teachings. But the different nuances could affect giving. In fact, they do, as Figure 6-27 reveals. While changing unjust social structures was the least likely response, members of parishes that emphasized that message contributed the most.

We also asked our pastors about their ecumenical teachings. Eighty-three percent indicated that they thought the Catholic Church was the one true church, while only 16% believed that other Christian faiths are equally valid. But, as shown in Figure 6-28, members of those parishes with the more ecumenical attitude contributed more.

Finally, we asked the pastors to compare their parish's teachings with those of a "typical" Catholic parish. Eighty percent said they were similar; 13% indicated that they allow more differences in interpreting Church teachings than other Catholic parishes; and 7% declared that they were probably stricter in interpreting Church teachings. Members of those parishes that allowed more flexibility in interpreting Church teachings tended to contribute more than the others, although the differences were not statistically significant.

The Pastor

Pastors can make a huge difference in the quality of parish life. There are legions of examples of cradle Catholics who left the Church because

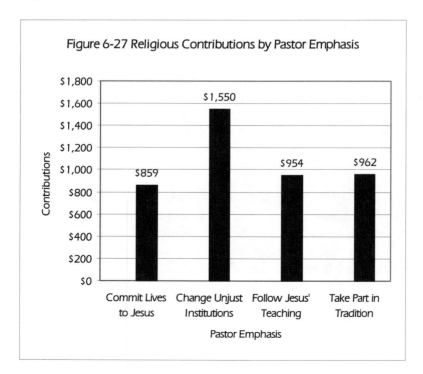

Figure 6-27 Religious Contributions by Pastor Emphasis

they disapproved of the way the pastor was running the parish. On the other hand, some pastors have built enormous reputations for their ability to almost single-handedly pull a parish through difficult times. A poor pastor can do a lot of damage. An excellent pastor can make up for a multitude of deficiencies in the other aspects of parish life. This fact is perhaps so obvious that few researchers have considered the pastor's impact on parish giving.

Michael Welch (1993), for example, did not directly ask parishioners about their opinions of their pastor. Rather, he asked about satisfaction with the quality of pastoral care in the parish. This would certainly include the contribution of the pastor, but would also include parishioners' ratings of associate pastors and lay staff. He found that there wasn't a significant relationship between this variable and parish giving.

An interesting twist on the role that pastors play can be found in a study done by Michael Cieslak (1994). He considered the effect on giving when a parish experienced a change in its pastor. This could either increase or decrease giving. The loss of a popular pastor might decrease contributions. The replacement of an unpopular pastor might increase

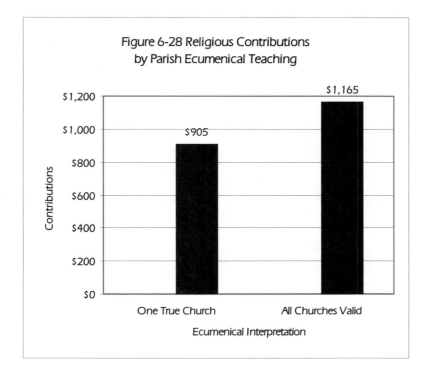

Figure 6-28 Religious Contributions by Parish Ecumenical Teaching

parish income. Cieslak studied the 106 parishes of the Rockford, Illinois, diocese during the period 1980 to 1993. He found that parishes did achieve a significant change in giving (either up or down) when a new pastor was appointed. The largest change tended to occur during a pastor's first year at his parish. The change in giving associated with the appointment of a new pastor was greatest in rural and suburban parishes, those with wealthier parishioners, parishes with younger members, those that did not have an elementary school (either on their own or a consolidated

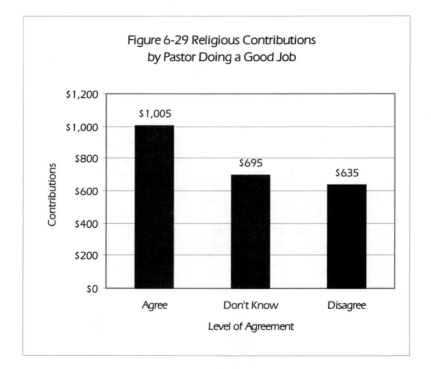

Figure 6-29 Religious Contributions
by Pastor Doing a Good Job

school), and those whose previous pastor had served at least 12 years. These results support the contention that a pastor can have an impact on parish giving.

What were our findings? For one thing, Catholic parishioners generally liked their pastor. About 87% either strongly or moderately agreed that their pastor had done a good job. This was in line with the other denominations in our sample. Did this matter? As Figure 6-29 illustrates, yes, it did. Parishioners who were more satisfied with their pastor contributed significantly more. Satisfaction with the pastors did make a difference!

The Bottom Line

Finally, we tried to gauge the degree to which Catholics' overall satisfaction with their parish affected their giving. This incorporates their rating of parish programs, their approval of parish decision-making processes, their agreement with any nuances in parish teachings, their sentiments about parish support for a parochial school, their feelings about their pastor, and their relationship with their fellow parishioners into one measure. This is obviously a complicated issue. To capture their attitude toward their parish, we asked them if they would feel a great sense of loss if for some reason they had to change parishes. Sixty-four percent either moderately or strongly agreed that they would. If this can be considered a measure of parish commitment, the Catholics in our sample were the least committed to their parish of any of the denominations that we studied. The Lutherans were almost as low (67%), but the others were well over 70%, with the Assemblies of God and Southern Baptists giving their congregations almost an 80% commitment rating.

Does this make a difference in religious contributions? It certainly does. In Figure 6-30 we can see that those who agreed that changing

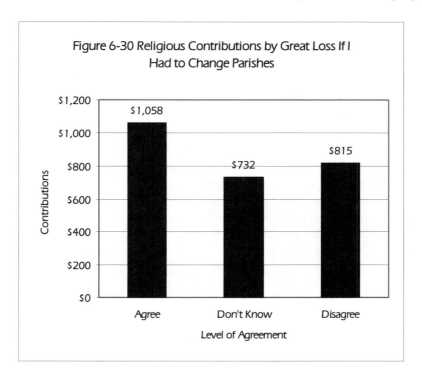

Figure 6-30 Religious Contributions by Great Loss If I Had to Change Parishes

parishes would be a big loss contributed significantly more than those who disagreed or were not sure.

A Word on Priestless Parishes

The vast majority of U.S. Catholic parishes are headed by a resident who serves as the pastor, often assisted by one or more priests serving in the role of parochial vicar, or assistant pastor. The shortage of priests in the United States (see Schoenherr and Young, 1993) has made it difficult for some dioceses to provide each parish with its own resident priest. These priestless parishes have typically been located in rural areas, although some have been established in inner cities.

A priestless parish is managed by a parish administrator, sometimes referred to as a lay pastor. This is frequently a woman religious, although other laypersons and ordained deacons also serve in this capacity. The parish is served by an ordained priest, who might visit the parish as seldom as once or twice a month. The lay pastor is not allowed to celebrate the Eucharist but instead presides at Communion services where hosts that were pre-consecrated by the visiting priest are distributed. The parish administrator provides many of the services that would be expected of an ordained priest, including preparation for the sacraments. However, the sacraments are administered by the visiting priest, except in those cases where the parish administrator is an ordained deacon. Deacons are authorized to administer baptisms, preside over marriages, and conduct funerals.

As one might expect, there are some problems with priestless parishes (see Gilmour, 1986, and Wallace, 1992). Frequently, a bishop's preparation of a parish for the assignment of a lay pastor has been inadequate. Tensions have arisen because of the role ambiguity between the lay pastor, who is responsible for preparing candidates for sacraments, and the visiting priest, who confers them. There have also been complaints from lay pastors that questions that should have been addressed to them have been inappropriately handled by the visiting priest.

A final problem with priestless parishes has been with the attitude of the parishioners. Some refuse to accept anyone (especially a woman) who serves in a role that they had come to expect would be filled by an ordained male. Also, they may feel that their parish has been downgraded and designated as "second class" if they haven't been assigned a priest on a full-time basis.

This doesn't mean that all priestless parishes are doomed to failure. We should recognize that the skills necessary to be an effective pastor are not automatically conferred at ordination, and many laypersons have been blessed with talents that would make them better pastors than some priests. Also, once a lay pastor has been given the chance to prove herself/himself, any reluctance on the part of parishioners to accept a lay pastor may dissipate.

D'Antonio et al. (1996) found that 55% of their respondents would find it acceptable if their parish structure included a lay parish administrator and a visiting priest. The same survey found that, in the event of a priest shortage, 70% of the respondents would consider Communion services led by laypersons using consecrated hosts to be an acceptable substitute for Sunday Mass (p. 177).

How do priestless parishes affect religious contributions? There were very few priestless parishes in our sample. As Figure 6-31 shows, households in priestless parishes contributed much less to their church than did households in parishes with a resident priest. Unfortunately, because of the small number of priestless parishes in our sample, these differences are not statistically significant. But they are striking, nevertheless. A word of caution is in order — we have a chicken or an egg problem in interpreting these findings. Are contributions low in priestless parishes

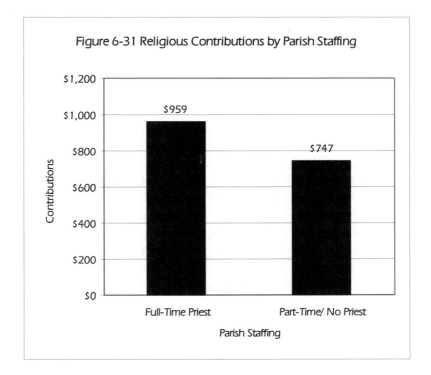

Figure 6-31 Religious Contributions by Parish Staffing

because of an absence of a resident priest? Or have these parishes been designated as priestless because of a variety of factors, including low contributions? Our data was not sufficiently detailed to answer these questions — we really need information on contributions before and after the parish was designated as priestless. All we can say for certain is that it appears that parishioners in parishes lacking a resident priest contribute less to their church.

Conclusions About the Role of the Parish

So what can we conclude about the effect of parish-specific factors on Catholic giving? First, contrary to the conventional wisdom, the large size of Catholic parishes is not the overriding factor in explaining low Catholic contributions. While it is true that members of large parishes contribute less, so do members of small parishes. Actually, medium-sized parishes (1,000-2,500 members) receive the largest contributions. Factors such as parish programs, liturgies, and preaching also tended not to be important.

Rather, parish decision-making processes tended to be critical in explaining contributions. Parishioners who feel that their parish leadership is accountable and trustworthy in financial matters, who feel that they are a part of the parish financial decision-making process, contribute more. But this desire for lay participation in parish decision-making extends into other areas beyond just parish finances. Parishioners who believe that other types of parish decisions are reached through open processes also contribute more. Clearly, the method of parish decisions being made because "Father said," will no longer work. This is not to say that priests aren't important. Parishioners who like their pastor contribute more. What it does mean is that those pastors who lead through a shared decision-making style are likely to be more successful, at least in generating parish contributions, than an autocratic pastor would be.

Parish schools are also important. We're able to confirm Greeley's findings that parishes that sponsor their own parochial schools receive larger contributions. But curiously, the benefits that a school provides to the parish do not seem to extend to co-sponsorship of a consolidated school. Parishes with consolidated schools actually receive lower contributions than do parishes with no school at all. Our findings are also consistent with another of Greeley's findings: parents of parochial school children contribute more than do parents who don't send their children to parochial schools. It might well be, as Greeley asserted, that Catholic schools pay for themselves!

Finally, one of the underlying themes of this book has been the tension between fund-raising and stewardship. We've been able to identify factors that would lead to larger contributions without requiring the change in mind-set associated with stewardship. But will the stewardship message work with Catholics? This chapter has shown that the answer is yes. Parishes that deliver a stewardship message receive larger contributions. Concerning the techniques involved in implementing that message, pledging was found to be successful, but other approaches, such as contacting members individually, were not.

Clearly, there are things that can be done at the parish level that will increase contributions without compromising fundamental Catholic Church teachings.

References

Cieslak, Michael J. "Changing Pastors: Does it Lead to a Change in Financial Contributions?" Unpublished paper presented at the 1994 Conference of the Religious Research Association.

Cieslak, Michael J. "Parish Responsiveness and Parish Commitment," *Review of Religious Research*, Vol. 26, No. 2 (December, 1984), pp. 132-47.

Gilmour, Peter. *The Emerging Pastor*. Kansas City: Sheed & Ward, 1986.

Greeley, Andrew and William McManus. *Catholic Contributions: Sociology and Policy*. Chicago: Thomas More Press, 1987.

Harris, Joseph Claude. "An Analysis of Catholic Sacrificial Giving Programs in Seattle, Washington," *Review of Religious Research*, Vol. 36, No. 2 (December, 1994), pp. 230-37.

Hoge, Dean R. and Boguslaw Augustyn. "Financial Contributions to Catholic Parishes: A Nationwide Study of Determinants," *Review of Religious Research*, Vol. 39, No. 1 (September, 1997), pp. 46-60.

National Conference of Catholic Bishops. "Stewardship: A Disciple's Response," Washington DC: U.S. Catholic Conference, 1993.

Oates, Mary J. *The Catholic Philanthropic Tradition in America*. Bloomington: Indiana University Press, 1995.

Rexhausen, Jeff and Michael J. Cieslak. "Relationship of Parish Characteristics to Sunday Giving Among Catholics in the Archdiocese of Cincinnati," *Review of Religious Research*, Vol. 36, No. 2 (December, 1994), pp. 218-29.

Schoenherr, Richard A. and Lawrence A. Young. *Full Pews and Empty Altars: Demographics of the Priest Shortage in United States Catholic Dioceses*. Madison: University of Wisconsin Press, 1993.

Wallace, Ruth A. *They Call Her Pastor: A New Role for Catholic Women.* Albany, NY: SUNY Press, 1992.

Welch, Michael R. "Participation and Commitment Among American Catholic Parishioners," in David A. Roozen and C. Kirk Hadaway (Eds.), *Church and Denominational Growth.* Nashville: Abingdon Press, 1993, pp. 324-45.

Zaleski, Peter A. and Charles E. Zech. "Economic and Attitudinal Factors in Catholic and Protestant Religious Giving," *Review of Religious Research*, Vol. 36, No. 2 (December, 1994), pp.158-67.

7

Generational Differences in Religious Giving

This is arguably one of the most contentious times in the history of the U.S. Catholic Church. As the National Pastoral Life Center's document *Called to Be a Catholic* described the situation, "it is widely admitted that the Catholic Church in the United States has entered a time of peril." The document went on to list 13 issues, including concerns over decision-making and consultation in church governance, the changing roles of women, the shortage of ordained clergy, and dwindling financial support, that caused its authors to reach this conclusion. It referred to "a mood of suspicion and acrimony (that) hangs over many of the most active in the Church's life" (*America*, 1996).

Attempts to understand the basis for these concerns can cut across a variety of dimensions. One popular approach has been Eugene Kennedy's (1995) dichotomy of Culture One and Culture Two Catholics that we described earlier. Briefly, Culture One Catholics view their Catholic faith from an institutional perspective. They place a great deal of reliance on the teaching authority of the Church, whether or not they happen to agree with a specific pronouncement. They actively participate in Church rituals and ceremonies, as well as in debates over the religious controversies of the day. Some might be classified as liberal on these issues while others would be considered conservative. But they share an affinity for the Church as an institution. As Kennedy points out, these are the lay Catholics that receive most of the media attention.

In contrast are the Culture Two Catholics. Like Culture One Catholics, Culture Two Catholics identify themselves as Catholic, regularly attend Mass, and recognize a role for the pope and clergy. They are not dissidents. But they place less reliance on the Church as an institution. Rather they look to the Church as a source of meaning as they go about their daily lives. For them the importance of the Church lies not in controversies over the ordination of women or the significance of the latest papal appointment. Rather, the Church's importance lies in the sacramental and pastoral support it provides as they cope with the joys and adversities of everyday life. Theirs is a much more personal, far less institutional, approach to religion.

While the Kennedy thesis has received quite a bit of attention, it doesn't really get to the issue of discord within the Church. Another dimension, that perhaps better explains the recent Church unrest, has been identified. This alternative approach views this "suspicion and acrimony" as a product of diverse perspectives held by the distinct generations that populate the U.S. Catholic Church today. According to this theory, the U.S. Catholic Church today consists of three separate generational cohorts, as we describe below.

Social scientists have long recognized the importance of "the formative years" in explaining human development. This is the period of late adolescence and young adulthood when social and political attitudes are formed. Some researchers believe the impressionable period starts as young as age 15, while others believe it extends to as late as age 25. Important events (such as the Great Depression, or a war) that individuals experience during their formative years establish their world views and have lifelong effects. Each generation shares not only a similar chronological age, but also a perception of society formed by its members' common experiences during their formative years.

Our interest here lies in how the events of individuals' formative period molded their religious attitudes and practices. Applying this theory to Catholic lay persons, the defining religious moment for the various generations of U.S. Catholics was the Second Vatican Council and the reforms that followed. Some Catholics (the pre-Vatican II cohort) experienced their formative years before Vatican II. Another group (the post-Vatican II cohort) was born in the late 1950s and later. Their formative years occurred after the reforms of Vatican II were in place. The middle generation (the Vatican II cohort) was permanently impacted by the occurrence of Vatican II during their formative years. These generations are somewhat analogous to the concepts of pre-baby boomers, baby boomers, and Generation X, except that many of those born during World War II would be included in the Vatican II cohort and the youngest baby boomers would be combined with the members of Generation X to form the post-Vatican II cohort.

The attitudes of each generation toward religion in general and specifically the Catholic Church are a reflection of both religious and societal occurrences during their formative years. Let's briefly review what some of these influences were and how they affected later religious attitudes.

The Pre-Vatican II Cohort

The dominant social events of any Americans who were raised in the 1930s and '40s were first the Great Depression and then World War II. Among the lessons they learned were the importance of cooperation in assisting each other economically and in pulling together to win a war. They came to trust institutional authorities and to rely on them to cope with economic adversity and to bring a peaceful settlement to international conflict. Authority was viewed as promoting the common good (Williams and Davidson, 1996, p. 275).

Catholics of this era tended to be either immigrants or the children of immigrants. They were frequently the victims of religious bigotry. To cope, they joined distinctively Catholic organizations. These organizations emphasized the importance of doctrinal orthodoxy and obeying Church teaching. In the words of Andrea Williams and James Davidson, "Catholics growing up in the 1930s and '40s were socialized into a 'ghetto mentality' which assumed that the world was a hostile place, and that Catholics would be safe if they stayed in the Church and participated in its large array of Catholic organizations. They learned a very collective, institutional approach to faith" (Williams and Davidson, 1996, p. 277).

In summary, pre-Vatican II Catholics were taught to love both their Church and their country. They learned to respect both religious and civil authority.

The Vatican II Cohort

In contrast to the pre-Vatican II generation, Catholics who grew up in the 1950s and '60s experienced two disparate, virtually contradictory eras, both in the secular and religious worlds. In the society at large, the 1950s were characterized by the calm of the Eisenhower administration. Authority and institutions still commanded respect. In contrast, the 1960s were characterized by an unpopular war, assassinations, and racial strife. All authority was questioned and challenged. Confidence in society's institutions diminished as they came to be viewed as part of the problem, not the solution.

By the 1960s, Catholics, riding the wave of the post-war economic expansion, had joined the middle class. They were now integrated into the mainstream of American society. The need for the security offered by the Church and the various Catholic organizations had been mitigated.

Dean Hoge, Benton Johnson, and Donald Luidens chronicled the social and cultural effects that impacted the religiosity of Protestant baby boomers in their book *Vanishing Boundaries* (1994). Most of these had an effect on Catholic baby boomers as well. For example, they cited the increase in liberal education among this generation. They argued that liberal education causes religious skepticism and relativism. Likewise, they noted that America had become increasingly pluralistic. The advent of television during this generation's childhood, along with increased travel, had exposed them to other cultures, in this case cultures beyond the "Catholic ghetto." This could weaken religious beliefs and commitment.

Two other, somewhat similar effects that Hoge et al., recognized were "individualism" and "privatism." The rise of self-centered individualism had weakened churchgoers' ties to their community, including their church. This could result in "faith without community," and leave one with the impression that church attendance, and indeed church authority, were optional. Privatism is a closely related concept. It refers to the tendency for Americans to settle in enclaves based on their common socioeconomic characteristics rather than a common history. These lifestyle enclaves value personal fulfillment rather than community. This includes religious beliefs. Religion is considered to be important only to the extent that it contributes to personal fulfillment.

Finally, Hoge et al., recognized the impact on baby boomers of the change in family structure. Besides the obvious impact of women's growing participation in the workplace, this also included cohabitation before marriage, the rising age of marriage with the corresponding delay in childbirth, and a rising divorce rate. Most religious denominations, not just the Catholic Church, have exhibited an inadequate response to these changes.

Members of this cohort were also exposed to some remarkable changes within the Catholic Church as well. As in the secular world, they are really a part of two different religious eras. In the 1950s they were raised much like the cohort that preceded them. They learned their religion from the *Baltimore Catechism*. They were taught a very institutional concept of religion: the Catholic Church was the "one true church." The unchallenged following of Church teaching was the only path to heaven.

In the 1960s, all of this changed dramatically. Suddenly, everything was turned upside-down. Rather than viewing the world as a hostile place, Catholics were now told that the Church had to become active in the world. Ecumenism replaced the emphasis on "the one true church." The hierarchical model of the Church was not totally discarded, but the laity was given new respect as "the people of God." They were told that through their baptism they shared in the priesthood. They were encouraged to get involved and make their voices heard through parish councils and other lay ministries.

Perhaps of most significance, the institutional emphasis of the Church was replaced by an emphasis on the importance of the individual. Again quoting Williams and Davidson, "At the same time that the Council was telling Catholics that traditions such as Latin Masses and meatless Fridays were no longer important, it was asking them to view their faith in more personal terms. Prior to Vatican II, Catholics were told to look first to the Church for guidance (an 'informed conscience' would be in agreement with Church teaching). The Council placed more emphasis on the integrity of one's conscience" (Williams and Davidson, 1996, p. 278).

This is consistent with the individualism and privatism that Hoge et al., had noted with regards to Protestant baby boomers.

But the Second Vatican Council wasn't the only earth-shattering religious experience that affected Catholics in the 1960s. In 1968, Pope Paul VI published his encyclical on artificial contraception, *Humanae Vitae*. It's safe to say that the encyclical was not met with unanimous acclaim by either the laity or the clergy. A large portion of married Catholics were already using some form of contraception. The report by the pope's own advisory committee, which had recommended that the birth-control decision be left to the individual couple, had been leaked to the public and had raised expectations about the pope's position. The documents of Vatican II had just declared the supremacy of individual conscience. Not only the laity, but many priests and some bishops, openly dissented with the pope. Some of the dissenting clergy were dealt with harshly. For the first time, many Catholics questioned the teaching authority of the Church (McNamara, 1993, p. 33).

So we see a generational cohort who, during their formative years, was struggling to mesh the respect for authority and institutions that they had learned in the 1950s with the disdain for authority and institutions that had become the hallmark of the 1960s. This was occurring in both their secular and religious lives. One result, as Wade Clark Roof

(1993) has pointed out, is that a large portion of them (in fact, two-thirds of the Catholics in his study) dropped out of church at one time or another. Most of those who dropped out did not return. Those who did return were permanently changed. For example, they preferred meditating alone over worshiping with others, and exploring different religions rather than learning more about their own faith.

The Post-Vatican II Cohort

The factors that Hoge et al., cited as affecting the religiosity of baby boomers came into full bloom during the formative years of the post-Vatican II generation. In addition, this cohort was raised in an era of cynicism toward both institutions and authority. In the secular world they experienced Watergate and Irangate, which reinforced the suspicion of government that had first emerged during the Vietnam war. They watched as national esteem for the United States' once-vaunted space program collapsed in light of the Challenger explosion and its aftermath. They saw the government seemingly paralyzed by its inability to deal with simultaneously high unemployment and inflation rates. They witnessed their parents or their friends' parents became innocent victims of a wave

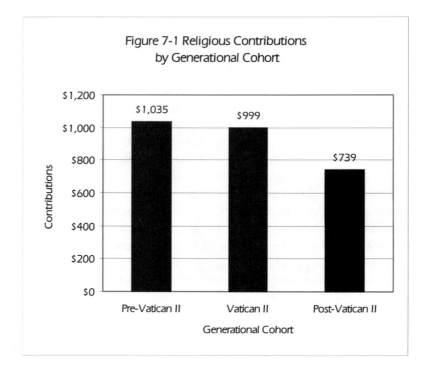

Figure 7-1 Religious Contributions by Generational Cohort

of corporate downsizing. On a religious level, they were exposed to stories of pedophilia and other misconduct among clergy.

Of course, by this time the reforms of Vatican II were in place. While members of this generation have little direct knowledge of Vatican II, they have felt its impact. They were not exposed to the *Baltimore Catechism*. Instead, personal responsibility for their own individual faith journey was emphasized. The Church was viewed as a tool for helping them get to heaven, rather than an end in itself. In fact, they likely place more importance on being a good Christian than on being a good Catholic. They feel free to disagree with Church teaching, often distinguishing between God's law and Church law. And they're more likely to consider the specific circumstances before determining the rightness or wrongness of an action (D'Antonio et al., pp. 84-88).

There is plenty of evidence that these different experiences during their impressionable years has had an important effect on the ways in which members of these generational cohorts perceive and practice their religion (See, for example, McNamara, 1993, and Davidson et al., 1997). But have these different experiences systematically affected their religious giving?

To answer this question, we first of all have to specify exactly whom we are including in each cohort. Remember, the data for this study was collected in 1993. Other studies have shown that giving drops off dramatically when people retire. Therefore, we're excluding from this analysis anyone born before 1928. As for the border between the pre-Vatican II cohort and the Vatican II generation, we chose the birth year of 1943. At the other end, we chose the boundary between the Vatican II cohort and the post-Vatican II group as the birth year 1958. We recognize that this latter boundary year is stretching things a bit as to the effect of the changes of the 1960s during their formative years, but we felt that people born in 1958 had more in common with those born before that year than those born after that year. In any event, whatever boundary years we chose would contain some degree of arbitrariness, and would be open to criticism.

It is also imperative that we recognize that religious giving by these different generations may differ because they are in different stages of their life cycles. The pre-Vatican II group is in their prime earning years, and most don't have to worry about saving to buy a home or to send their children to college. The Vatican II generation, on the other hand, is saving for college, paying off a mortgage, and have yet to reach their best earning years. The post-Vatican II cohort is just beginning, struggling to save for a home or pay a mortgage, starting a family, and earning at or just beyond entry-level incomes. It is no surprise then that, as Figure 7-1 indicates, the pre-Vatican II households in our sample contribute the most, followed by the Vatican II and then the post-Vatican II generations. To account for this in the analysis that follows, we divided each household's contributions by their cohort's average contributions. That allows us to determine whether each determinant that we study leads to above-average or below-average contributions for that cohort by calculating a cohort index. In the figures that follow, a cohort index of 100 indicates giving right at the cohort average. An index less than 100 signifies religious contributions below the cohort average, while a value greater than 100 demonstrates giving at levels above the cohort average.

First, we can identify the areas in which there was no significant effect on religious giving. These include the so-called pelvic issues (Church teachings on abortion, birth control, and the ordination of women) as well as denominational programs and policies. Members of the different cohorts may not agree with one another on Church teachings, the quality of Church programs, or various Church policies. But their differences did not translate into significant differences in giving across the cohorts.

The results at the parish level were quite different. Here, we found that differences in attitudes among the cohorts resulted in differences in giving in two specific realms: parish decision-making and pledging.

Cohorts and Parish Decision-Making Processes

We saw earlier that parish decision-making processes had a significant effect on giving. In general, we have shown that parishioners who felt that they had both information about and input into parish decisions contributed more. But does this vary by generational cohort? The answer is yes. We asked our sample if they felt they had enough information about the handling and allocation of parish funds. Figure 7-2 shows that all three cohorts exhibited a drop-off in giving when they were dissatisfied with the amount of financial information that they were given, but the greatest decrease (27%) was experienced by the post-Vatican II group. We had also asked if they thought that typical parishioners had enough influence in parish financial decisions. Among those who indicated that they did not, both the pre-Vatican II group and the post-Vatican II group contributed less than their cohorts' average (actually, a lot less for the post-Vatican II cohort), but the Vatican II group's contributions actually exceeded their cohort's average (Figure 7-3). The pattern of the Vatican II cohort reacting in an opposite fashion from the other

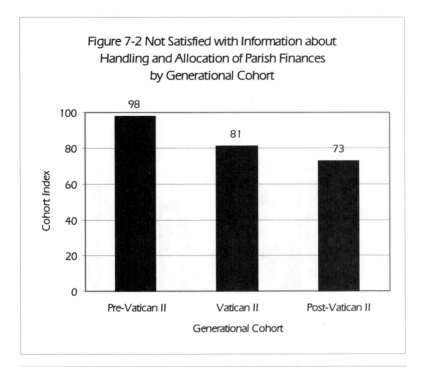

Figure 7-2 Not Satisfied with Information about Handling and Allocation of Parish Finances by Generational Cohort

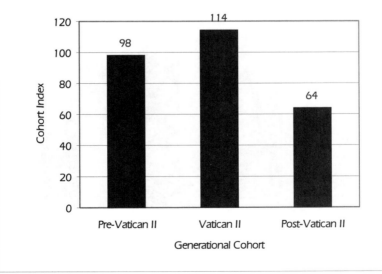

Figure 7-3 Don't Feel that Parishoners Have Enough Influence in Use of Church Funds by Generational Cohort

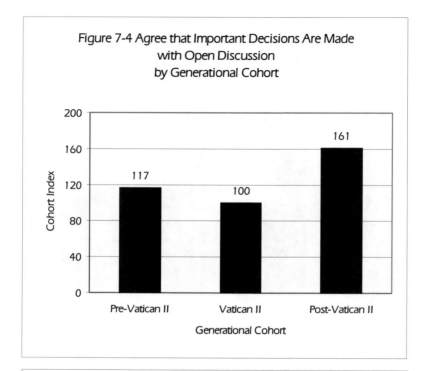

Figure 7-4 Agree that Important Decisions Are Made with Open Discussion by Generational Cohort

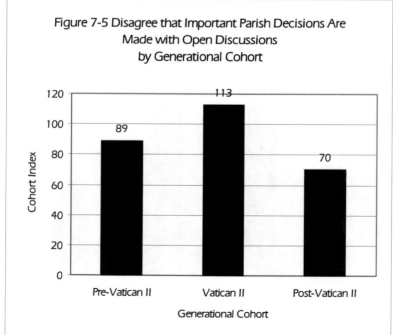

Figure 7-5 Disagree that Important Parish Decisions Are Made with Open Discussions by Generational Cohort

two generations is one that occurs frequently, as we'll see throughout this chapter. It is probably symptomatic of the confusion that this cohort feels as a result of its bridging two very different periods in both secular and Church history.

An interesting pattern emerged when we shifted gears and asked about parish decision-making in general. We saw earlier that those who thought that important parish decisions were made after open discussion contributed more. But of that group, the Vatican II generation just contributed at their cohort's average, while the other two groups contributed above their cohort's average (Figure 7-4). In fact, the post-Vatican II group who experienced open discussion in their parish contributed 61% more than the average for their cohort. At the other extreme, those who did not find open discussion in their parish decision-making contributed less. But as Figure 7-5 shows, when we broke this down by generational cohort, the Vatican II group who did not experience open discussion actually contributed more. The pre-Vatican II group contributed 11% less, and the post-Vatican II group gave 30% less than their respective cohort averages.

What can we conclude about the effect of parish decision-making processes on giving across the three cohorts? First, the Vatican II generation is erratic. Their giving often moves in a pattern counter to the other two cohorts. This could be the result, as mentioned earlier, of confusion among members of this cohort brought about by their bridging of two such dissimilar time periods. The other pattern that emerges is how emphatically open decision-making processes affect the post-Vatican II generation. Their giving drops dramatically (27% to 36% below cohort average) when open processes are not in place, but rises just as dramatically (61% above cohort average) when they are.

Cohorts and Pledging

Earlier we found that members of parishes where pledging is encouraged contribute more. Does this pattern vary by generational cohort? Yes. Figure 7-6 shows that there are significant generational differences in parishes that do not employ pledge cards. The pre-Vatican II and post-Vatican II cohorts are similar. Their members contribute 22% and 23% less, respectively, than their individual cohort averages. Once again, members of the Vatican II generation are an anomaly as they contribute at a rate slightly above cohort average when their parish doesn't use pledge cards. But for those who disapprove of the practice of pledging, members of all three groups contribute below their respective cohort averages (Figure 7-7). The same is true among those who either failed to complete a pledge card or weren't certain (Figure 7-8). In both cases, the largest drop-off from average giving in the cohort came with the post-Vatican II generation.

Conclusions

There is strong evidence to support the hypothesis that the U.S. Catholic Church today is populated by three distinct generations. Patrick McNamara (1993) and James Davidson et al. (1997) have convincingly demonstrated that these generational cohorts not only exist, but differ from one another significantly in their religious attitudes and practices. Briefly, the pre-Vatican II generation takes an institutional view towards the Church. When they think of the Church, they think of a hierarchical, authoritarian organization whose primary function is to serve as a mediating force between them and God. They have a great deal of respect for the Church's teaching authority. In contrast, the post-Vatican II cohort views religion as more personal and individualistic. When they think of the Church, they think of themselves. They are the "people of God." They are on a faith journey, and organized religion exists merely to sup-

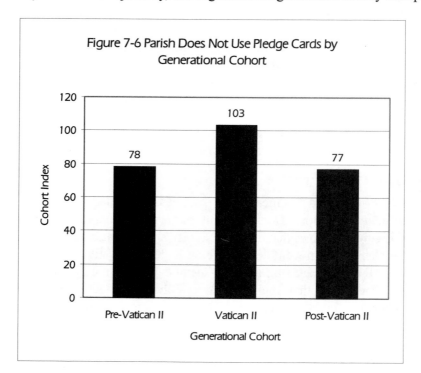

Figure 7-6 Parish Does Not Use Pledge Cards by Generational Cohort

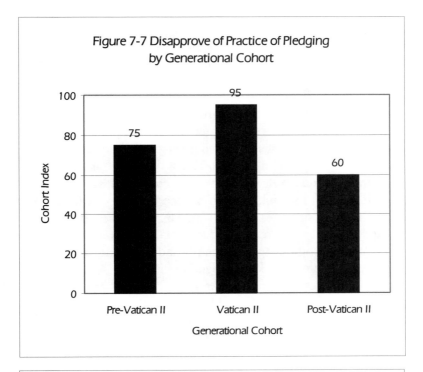

Figure 7-7 Disapprove of Practice of Pledging by Generational Cohort

Figure 7-8 Failed to Fill Out Pledge Card by Generational Cohort

port that journey. They expect a more democratic structure, one in which they are involved in nearly every aspect of Church life. The Vatican II generation is a transition group that has a foot in both camps. They spent their early years in a pre-Vatican II, institutional church, but came of age in a post-Vatican II, individualistic church.

This chapter has shown that many of these differences carry over in their impact on religious giving. In general, we found that the Vatican II generation is unpredictable. Their religious giving frequently is affected in a completely opposite manner than that of other Catholics. Perhaps schizophrenia is too strong a word to use here, but clearly this cohort is far less unified in its thinking than are the members of the other two groups. Given the struggles that we would expect this cohort to have had in trying to blend and make sense of two totally different secular (1950s and 1960s) and religious (pre-Vatican II and post-Vatican II) eras, perhaps this outcome isn't so surprising after all.

Another unexpected trend that we found was the virtually complete agreement between the pre-Vatican II and post-Vatican II cohorts in their giving reactions. The same factors resulted in their giving at levels greater than their cohort average in some instances, and less than their cohort average in others. Having said this, though, we should note that the post-Vatican II cohort exhibited much larger swings in their giving. When factors occurred that they did not approve of (such as the lack of open parish decision-making), their contributions dipped much more than the other groups. But when factors occurred for which they expressed approval (such as the existence of open parish discussion), their giving rose much more rapidly than that of the others.

References

America. "Called to be Catholic: Church in a Time of Peril," August 31, 1996, pp. 5-8.

D'Antonio, William V., James D. Davidson, Dean R. Hoge, and Ruth A. Wallace. *Laity: American and Catholic.* Kansas City: Sheed & Ward, 1996.

Davidson, James D. et al. *The Search for Common Ground: What Unites and Divides Catholic Americans.* Huntington, IN: Our Sunday Visitor Publishing, 1997.

Hoge, Dean R., Benton Johnson, and Donald A. Luidens. *Vanishing Boundaries.* Louisville: Westminster/John Knox Press, 1994.

Kennedy, Eugene. *Tomorrow's Catholics, Yesterday's Church.* Liguori, MO: Triumph Books, 1995.

McNamara, Patrick. *Conscience First, Tradition Second.* Albany: SUNY Press, 1993.

Roof, Wade Clark. *A Generation of Seekers.* San Francisco: Harper, 1993.

Williams, Andrea S. and James D. Davidson. "Catholic Conceptions of Faith: A Generational Analysis." *Sociology of Religion*, 57 (3): 273-89, 1996.

8

Seven Things the Catholic Church Can Do to Increase Contributions

We've analyzed a variety of determinants of religious contributions. Some have a significant effect on religious contributions, while others do not. Some are within the control of the Church, while others, such as personal characteristics, are not. Of those over which the Church has control, some, because of theological and ecclesiastical reasons, cannot be changed. But that still leaves a broad range of factors that the Church can address if it is serious about increasing parishioners' financial commitment.

The actions that we recommend are listed in the order that we think would be most effective. This ranking was developed from the information presented in the previous chapters, supplemented with some additional information gathered from a statistical procedure called multiple-regression analysis. We don't want to bore the reader with a detailed discussion of this procedure here. Briefly, up to this point we have looked at the factors one at a time, without concern for the simultaneous impact of any other factors. But researchers like to assess the independent effect of each variable. Multiple-regression analysis allows us to control for the effect of other variables while singling out the impact of a specific factor. For example, we might want to hone in on just the issue of how parishioners' opinion of their pastor affects their giving. By using multiple-regression analysis, we can isolate on this one relationship. The effect of other determinants of religious giving, such as income or attitude towards birth control, will have been controlled for and thus eliminated. When other variables are controlled, the effect of each factor can be expected to diminish, partly because the different variables tend to overlap with one another. This method serves to reinforce any findings from considering each factor separately.

So here are our recommendations, ranked in order of importance. We anticipate that some will disagree with our rank ordering. But there should be no controversy over the importance of addressing each of these issues.

1. Develop Stewardship

The one best thing the Church should do if it is serious about increasing giving among Catholics is to instill a sense of stewardship among its members. This is not only a practical solution, with enormous financial benefits, it is also theologically sound. In fact, stewardship is so theologically sound that it probably should be emphasized even if the Church wasn't interested in raising more money. This holistic approach invites renewal at both the individual and parish level. But to be effective, it cannot be considered a fringe activity. It has been said that, "The Church is good at developing stewardship programs, but not stewards." Stewardship must be at the center of parish life. Parishes must make significant changes in their orientation. All parish activities and programs need to be evaluated in terms of their impact in developing a community of stewards.

But, as we cautioned earlier, stewardship must go beyond the mere raising of money. The emphases on the time and talent dimensions are at least as critical as the emphasis on treasure. That's why tithing, although attractive, is not one of our suggestions. Because of its narrow focus, tithing does not offer the opportunity for renewal that stewardship does. As an aside, we might note that the value of time contributed to a Church also has a significant monetary value (Zech et al., 1997).

This is not the place for a step-by-step guide on how to implement stewardship in the parish. That has already been done, and done very well. Among the best are *Stewardship: Disciples Respond*, a guidebook put out by the National Catholic Stewardship Council; *Stewardship by the Book*, published by Sheed & Ward; and *The 'M' Word: Money, Mission, Ministry*, published by Chicago Studies. But some of the techniques of stewardship that we studied seemed to work better than others.

Pledging

As we mentioned above, pledging was not a very popular concept among participants in our focus groups. But what does it say about a community of people who will make multi-year commitments to purchase automobiles, vacation homes, boats, etc., but refuse to make a yearly commitment to their church? What do they own, and what owns them? Where are their treasures and their hearts? Aside from the sound theological arguments for asking people to make a commitment to their church, the simple truth is that pledging works. People who pledge are better givers. People who plan their religious giving on an annual basis, rather than by looking at their checkbook each Sunday to see what they can afford that week, contribute more. Incidentally, most stewardship programs urge the parish to ask for a commitment of time and talent as well as treasure.

Other Stewardship Techniques

There are other techniques besides pledging that most stewardship programs recommend. These include homilies on stewardship by pastors, laypersons' testimonials on what stewardship has meant in their lives, and contacting parishioners directly, either in person or by telephone. We found that none of these significantly increased Catholic contributions. This is not to say that they hurt contributions, or that they shouldn't be used. But they don't have the impact that the literature put out by the various stewardship programs would lead us to believe. Perhaps as Catholics become more comfortable with the idea of stewardship, these techniques will have a greater impact.

Finally, while every study has concluded that Catholics contribute less than most Protestant denominations, most have also shown that the greatest shortfall is among the wealthier Catholics. Any parish-wide stewardship program must make a special effort to ensure that the stewardship message touches this group. A similar pattern emerges among the most committed members, those who attend worship services at least once a week. Again, the giving of this group of Catholics lags far behind the Protestants in our sample.

In developing their stewardship message, parishes can't forget their most committed members.

2. Parish Decision-Making Processes

We asked the question in a number of different ways, and each time the answer came out the same. Parishioners want more say about how their parishes are run. This extends beyond merely being informed about what's happening. They want to be consulted and have direct input into decision-making processes. In parish financial matters they expect accountability. This can only be assured when the laity (through their representation on parish finance committees and parish councils) have an input into both the development and the approval of the parish budget. The laity also expect to play a role in the non-financial matters of the parish. They want open discussion of parish issues. Situations where all decisions are made by the pastor or a small clique of parishioners (either appointed by the pastor or self-appointed) only serve to discourage parishioners, with a predictable effect on their giving.

In many respects, shared parish decision-making is just an extension of stewardship. One effective way of instilling a sense of stewardship in people is to develop in them an attitude of ownership of the resources over which they are stewards. Jesus himself spoke of the relationship between stewardship and ownership/responsibility (see Matthew 25:14-30; Luke 19:12-27). It would be difficult to develop a parish of stewards if all parish decision-making has been taken out of their hands. At best, this would leave parishioners with a very incomplete and immature sense of stewardship.

We should observe that the importance of shared decision-making occurs primarily at the parish level. Catholics are less certain of the importance of shared decision-making at the denominational level. Those who approve of the current breakdown in decision-making between the denomination and the parish contribute more. So do those who feel they already receive enough information about denominational handling of funds, as do those who approve of the denomination's decision-making processes. There is evidence that contention over decision-making processes at the parish level affects contributions. The evidence at the denominational level is not so clear-cut.

3. Parish Size

The extraordinarily large membership in Catholic parishes, compared to the much smaller congregations of most Protestant churches, is not the overwhelming drag on Catholic contributions that most other studies would lead us to believe. Some have found it to be the single most important factor in explaining low contributions among Catholics. It's not. But it's still important. Excessively large Catholic parishes rob parishioners of a sense of parish community. This is vital to parish life as a whole, not just to religious contributions. Large parishes also increase the tendency towards free-riding.

But we found that small parishes are no better. As to why, we can only speculate. It might be their inability to sustain parish programs that appeal to particular parishioner needs. Perhaps it's easier in small parishes for a small clique of parishioners to dominate and deprive others of a sense of ownership. Maybe it's related to their inability to support a parish school. In any event, in the case of parishes, it's not necessarily true that "small is beautiful."

Our finding, supported by some others, is that medium-sized parishes (1,000-2,500 members) receive the largest contributions. While still large by Protestant standards, parishes in this range are large enough to support an array of programs that Catholics value (including a parochial school) but small enough so that an effective pastor can inspire a sense of ownership and community among parishioners.

While there may be sound pastoral reasons for maintaining small parishes (in order to preserve a presence in the inner city, for example), we can think of no justification, either pastoral or financial, for allowing parishes to rise above 2,500 members.

4. Parochial Schools

In many instances, the findings reported in this book are in disagreement with the pioneering work on this topic done by Andrew Greeley. This is most notably true with respect to our findings on the effect of Church teachings on sexual ethics. But one issue where we are in agreement with Greeley is the effect of parochial schools on giving. Parents who send their children to parochial schools contribute more than do other parents of school-aged children. It might be tempting to dismiss this finding by claiming that this is just another measure of commitment, like church attendance. If that were the case, then we couldn't claim any cause-effect relationship between parochial schools and religious giving. But we also found that, overall, members of parishes that sponsor their own parochial school contribute more than others. Our data doesn't tell us if these higher contributions are in response to the spiritual and/or social impact that the school has on the parish. Maybe this pattern merely reflects the response by parishioners to a financial need inherent in supporting a school. But whatever the reason, members of parishes with their own parochial schools are more generous in their religious contributions.

Surprisingly, the effect of the school on parishioners' contributions doesn't transfer to a parish that co-sponsors a consolidated school. Not only are consolidated schools associated with lower giving than parishes with their own parochial school, but members of these parishes actually contribute less than those in parishes with no school at all. Whatever benefits a parish-sponsored parochial school provides are quickly dissipated when parishes merge schools. In this era of tight budgets and declining parochial-school enrollments, consolidated schools are an attractive alternative. Our results should serve to caution parishes from moving too quickly in that direction. Much is lost when a parish relinquishes control over its own school.

We don't mean to imply here that merely starting a parochial school will automatically increase contributions. We wish it were that simple. We're not even sure that we can agree with Greeley's assertion that parochial schools pay for themselves in the form of higher contributions. What we do know is that a parochial school is a valuable asset. Parishes that already have a school should recognize its potential. A parish that properly uses this resource to enhance parish spirituality and community will be a better parish. One likely outcome will be larger contributions. Parishes that don't have a school have to find some other activity that the parish can rally around in order to generate the same sort of benefits as a school.

5. Teachings

No one would suggest that the Catholic Church, or any religion, should modify its teachings in order to increase contributions. But within the range of acceptable Church theology and ecclesiology, some teachings have been shown to have a greater impact on giving than others. These could receive special emphasis.

One of these is the message of ecumenism. Our results show that members of parishes that proclaim a more ecumenical message contribute more. Likewise, those parishioners who disagree with the notion that only followers of Jesus can be saved contribute more. With the Vatican II emphasis on reaching out to our Protestant and non-Christian neighbors, there is a happy marriage between what the Church is urging parishes to do anyway and increased religious contributions.

Another type of message that was associated with larger giving concerned the primary duty of Christians. Here, two separate themes stood out as attracting greater contributions. One was an emphasis on Church traditions and sacraments. The Catholic Church is, at its core, a sacramental Church. Likewise, much of our faith is based on tradition. These are orthodox teachings that Catholics still cherish and respond to financially. The other teaching was concerned with changing unjust social structures. This is a more modern, post-Vatican II concept. Yet, it too is one that elicits a financial response from Catholics.

In contrast to the findings of Andrew Greeley, we've found the Church's teachings on sexual ethics (specifically abortion and birth control) haven't alienated Catholics to the extent of affecting their religious contributions. In fact, those who support the Church's position on these issues are better givers. The only exception is the ordination of women, where those who disagree with the Church's position contribute more.

6. Remind People that the Church Needs Their Contributions

Purists who emphasize a stewardship message cringe at the thought of using church need as an argument for raising money. Yet, the fact of the matter is that many Catholics believe that their Church is wealthy and doesn't need their financial support. They look at the Church's vast land holdings and other assets, and wonder why their contributions are necessary. Others, aware that their clergy is celibate, and that many have taken a vow of poverty, wonder why the Church's financial needs are more pressing than those of their own household. And others, cognizant of the Church's large membership (internationally, nationally, and locally) don't think that their contributions will be missed and become free-riders.

But the fact of the matter is that the Church, in spite of its enormous asset holdings, inexpensive (clergy) labor, and large membership, does need our contributions to maintain itself and to expand its ministries. That message must get through. Our findings show that Catholics who believe that the Church has serious financial needs contribute more. This is true at both the denominational and parish level. This is the antithesis of the stewardship message. But a stewardship campaign will never be fully effective in increasing religious contributions unless parishioners are convinced of the Church's need for their donations. Otherwise, they might choose to practice their stewardship by contributing to worthwhile causes other than their religion.

7. Meet the Special Needs of Parishioners

Parishes are generally formed around geographic boundaries. In many cases, this means that members have a similar socioeconomic status. But this doesn't mean that a parish should be viewed as a monolith. In many instances their similar socioeconomic status masks a population with diverse needs from their parish. Parishes need to stand ready to meet these needs. Those that are the most successful will probably enjoy larger contributions. Our results show that, while we couldn't single out any one parish program that leads to higher contributions, members who were more satisfied with their parish contributed more.

This is not a particularly startling revelation. But we'd like to point out one group that requires special parish attention. These are the young adults, the Generation X-ers, who will soon be the leaders of the Church. We saw in the previous chapter that this group has a different set of religious needs and aspirations than earlier generations. As much as parishioners in general want involvement in parish decision-making processes, members of this generation are even more so inclined. This penchant for lay control extends to other aspects of Church life, such as selecting their own pastor. They are more likely to believe in the primacy of individual conscience over Church teachings. To many, it is more important to be a good Christian than it is to be a good Catholic.

And they feel less of an obligation to support their Church financially.

This is a radically different way of thinking about the Catholic Church. It is a permanent shift in attitude, not just a "stage" that they are going through. It is important that the Church make whatever adjustments it can within theologically acceptable limits to accommodate this cohort. The impact of this cohort's approach to religion extends far beyond mere financial implications. Like stewardship, this is such an important issue that it must be addressed, even if there were no financial benefits. But the fact that this cohort will be the primary financial supporters of the Church throughout the first third of the next century only serves to make it more critical.

Another group that warrants special attention comprises the adult parishioners (single, widowed, and divorced or separated) who do not have children living at home. These households are among the Church's better givers, but they are often forgotten as parishes gear their programs and resources towards children.

Conclusion

Throughout this chapter, and in fact, throughout this book, there has run an undercurrent of tension between the theological message of stewardship and the practical elements of fund-raising. In many ways the two are at odds. Fund-raising is what we do; stewardship is who we are. Fund-raising is one-dimensional, impacting only people's checkbooks;

stewardship invites us to change our hearts. Fund-raising typically occurs annually, in conjunction with financing the parish budget; stewardship is an ongoing commitment.

By placing stewardship as our number-one recommendation, it should be clear to the reader where we stand on this issue. Yet, we recognize a role for both. It is difficult for us to imagine a successful stewardship campaign, no matter how well-thought-out or theologically grounded, occurring in a parish where the laity don't feel a part of the decision-making process, where they don't feel a sense of ownership for the parish, where the parish is too large to develop a sense of community, and where they aren't inspired by the parish teachings. Furthermore, if the parishioners are convinced that the Church is financially well-off and doesn't need their money, a successful stewardship program could actually serve to reduce religious contributions, as parishioners search out other worthwhile causes to live their stewardship through.

In short, these other recommendations should be viewed as pre-conditions to successful parish stewardship. Stewardship is primary, but without these other factors in place, any stewardship program will, at a minimum, be less effective than it could be, and may even be doomed to failure.

References

Zech, Charles E., Patrick McNamara, and Dean R. Hoge. "Lagging Stewards, Part Two: Catholics as Church Volunteers," *America*, February 8, 1997, pp. 21-25.

Responses to Congregation Profiles

This appendix gives the percentage responses to the items asked in the Congregation Profiles. There were 125 congregations in each denomination. All the data were weighted to represent a random sample of congregations in each denomination. Columns may not total to 100 because of rounding.

Q2. When was the congregation founded?

	AOG	SBC	CATH	LUTH	PRES
Before 1900	0	34	36	47	57
1900-1949	36	26	33	15	21
1950-1979	36	28	29	35	19
1980 or later	28	12	2	3	3

Q3. Which of the following best describes the pastoral staff situation of your congregation during the last complete fiscal year?

	AOG	SBC	CATH	LUTH	PRES
At least one full-time pastor	95	89	93	84	87
Part-time pastor	5	9	7	13	13
Position temporarily vacant	1	3	0	4	0

Q4. Number of members

	AOG	SBC	CATH	LUTH	PRES
1 to 100	32	22	0	16	26
101 to 250	37	41	6	40	35
251 to 500	20	20	10	30	25
501 to 1,000	8	14	16	10	10
1,001 to 2,500	4	4	26	4	4
2,501 to 5,000	0	1	23	0	1
5,001 to 10,000	0	0	18	0	0

Q6. Number of households

	AOG	SBC	CATH	LUTH	PRES
1 to 100	74	57	7	42	43
101 to 250	19	23	13	42	42
251 to 500	3	14	20	12	10
501 to 1,000	3	5	22	2	4
1,001 to 2,500	1	1	29	2	1
2,501 to 5,000	0	0	9	0	1
5,001 to 10,000	0	0	1	0	0

Q7. What was the average worship attendance on a typical weekend? Give total for all worship services. Persons attending more than once should be counted only once.

	AOG	SBC	CATH	LUTH	PRES
1 to 100	50	53	3	51	52
101 to 250	37	31	9	34	35
251 to 500	8	12	15	13	10
501 to 1,000	5	4	25	2	3
1,001 to 2,500	1	1	36	0	1
2,501 to 5,000	0	0	10	0	0
5,001 to 10,000	0	0	1	0	0

Q8. Where is your congregation located?

	AOG	SBC	CATH	LUTH	PRES
Large city (over 250,000)	18	16	15	13	21
Suburb of large city	14	13	9	8	20
Medium city (under 250,000)	14	8	12	12	9
Suburb of medium city	3	2	5	5	3
Small city (10,000 to 49,000)	24	10	22	12	13
Town (2,500 or more)	14	8	20	12	14
Town (2,500 or less)	5	12	14	18	14
Rural	9	32	4	20	7

Q9. What percent of your members are female?

	AOG	SBC	CATH	LUTH	PRES
0 - 20	0	0	0	0	0
21 - 40	0	3	1	2	2
41 - 60	73	76	93	85	66
61 - 80	27	20	6	11	32
81 - 10	0	0	1	0	2

Q10. Age:
18 - 24 years old

	AOG	SBC	CATH	LUTH	PRES
0 - 20	83	95	922	95	95
21 - 40	16	4	8	5	6
41 - 60	1	1	0	0	0

25 - 39 years old

	AOG	SBC	CATH	LUTH	PRES
0 - 20	21	38	42	38	38
21 - 40	58	52	55	58	56
41 - 60	14	9	2	4	6
61 - 80	6	2	1	0	1
81 - 10	1	0	72	71	63
41 - 60	20	11	13	4	3
61 - 80	0	1	1	0	1

60 - 75 years old

	AOG	SBC	CATH	LUTH	PRES
0 - 20	76	52	61	45	41
21 - 40	20	41	33	47	48
41 - 60	5	6	4	8	11
61 - 80	0	1	1	0	0

>75 years old

	AOG	SBC	CATH	LUTH	PRES
0 - 20	99	93	95	90	81
21 - 40	1	7	5	10	16
41 - 60	0	0	0	0	3

Q11. What percent of your members are:
African-American

	AOG	SBC	CATH	LUTH	PRES
0 - 20	97	96	99	99	93
21 - 40	1	0	0	0	3
41 - 60	0	0	0	1	0
61 - 80	0	0	0	0	0
81 - 100	2	4	1	0	4

Asian

	AOG	SBC	CATH	LUTH	PRES
0 - 20	99	100	97	100	100
21 - 40	1	0	1	0	0
61 - 80	0	0	1	0	0

Hispanic

	AOG	SBC	CATH	LUTH	PRES
0 - 20	88	99	91	100	99
21 - 40	4	1	5	0	1
41 - 60	1	0	2	0	0
61 - 80	1	0	0	0	0
81 - 100	7	0	2	0	0

American-Indian

	AOG	SBC	CATH	LUTH	PRES
0 - 20	99	97	100	96	100
21 - 40	1	0	0	0	0
41 - 60	0	0	0	0	0
61 - 80	0	1	0	0	0
81 - 10	0	0	2	0	1

White

	AOG	SBC	CATH	LUTH	PRES
0 - 20	10	7	6	1	4
21 - 40	1	0	1	0	0
41 - 60	3	0	4	1	0
61 - 80	7	4	5	2	4
81 - 100	79	89	84	97	92

Others

	AOG	SBC	CATH	LUTH	PRES
0 - 20	99	100	100	100	100
21 - 40	1	0	0	0	0
41 - 60	0	0	0	0	0
61 - 80	0	0	0	0	0
81 - 100	1	0	0	0	0

Q12. What percent of your members have:
College degree

	AOG	SBC	CATH	LUTH	PRES
0 - 20	69	54	41	51	24
21 - 40	20	27	40	26	24
41 - 60	9	12	14	9	25
61 - 80	2	7	6	13	19
81 - 100	0	1	0	1	9

High-school diploma

	AOG	SBC	CATH	LUTH	PRES
0 - 20	6	6	3	3	15
21 - 40	8	13	19	17	24
1 - 60	18	25	62	23	29
61 - 80	40	43	31	47	25
81 - 100	28	13	7	11	8

<High-school diploma

	AOG	SBC	CATH	LUTH	PRES
0 - 20	85	79	87	83	95
21 - 40	9	14	10	15	4
41 - 60	1	3	3	1	0
61 - 80	5	3	0	1	1
81 - 100	5	1	0	0	0

Q13. What percent of your members would you estimate have household incomes of:
<20,000

	AOG	SBC	CATH	LUTH	PRES
0 - 20	50	57	56	52	67
21 - 40	21	21	28	30	14
41 - 60	13	9	8	11	8
61 - 80	8	8	7	5	9
81 - 100	8	6	1	3	3

20,000 - 50,000

	AOG	SBC	CATH	LUTH	PRES
0 - 20	11	10	8	8	8
21 - 40	14	18	19	22	24
41 - 60	30	23	38	37	34
61 - 80	29	40	28	29	28
81 - 100	16	10	8	5	6

50,000 - 100,000

	AOG	SBC	CATH	LUTH	PRES
0 - 20	89	78	71	68	59
21 - 40	9	19	23	25	86
41 - 60	1	3	5	6	11
61 - 80	1	1	1	1	2

>100,000

	AOG	SBC	CATH	LUTH	PRES
0 - 20	100	100	100	100	97
21 - 40	0	0	0	0	3

Q14. What organized groups did your congregation sponsor last year?

	AOG	SBC	CATH	LUTH	PRES
Children Sunday school	98	99	99	94	97
Youth Sunday school	92	99	90	84	90
Adult Sunday school	98	100	53	79	87
Prayer group (church)	95	95	65	66	75
Prayer group (home)	43	23	30	43	35
Singles group	24	30	14	5	10
Men's groups	58	54	57	24	36
Women's group	84	82	81	90	93
Senior adult's group	31	47	45	32	48
Youth group	92	81	75	64	79
Children's group	91	70	47	39	49
Music program	55	58	34	37	52
Other	52	65	34	27	43

Q15. Did your congregation operate a parochial (five-day-a-week) school last year? (Do not include day-care center, preschool, or before- or after-school "latchkey" programs.)

	AOG	SBC	CATH	LUTH	PRES
Yes	8	0	39	2	1
No	92	0	61	98	99

Q16. Did your congregation co-sponsor, with other congregations, a parochial school?

	AOG	SBC	CATH	LUTH	PRES
Yes	2	0	30	0	0
No	98	100	70	100	100

Q17. Did your congregation sponsor a day care center or preschool?

	AOG	SBC	CATH	LUTH	PRES
Yes	9	10	35	18	30
No	92	91	65	82	70

Q18. Did your congregation sponsor a before- or after-school "latchkey" program?

	AOG	SBC	CATH	LUTH	PRES
Yes	5	3	21	6	9
No	96	97	79	94	91

Q19. Is space in your facility used, rent-free, for any community social programs?

	AOG	SBC	CATH	LUTH	PRES
Yes	34	42	75	76	81
No	66	58	25	24	19

Q20. Did your congregation sponsor or support at least one missionary last year?

	AOG	SBC	CATH	LUTH	PRES
Yes	97	52	66	30	54
No	3	48	34	70	46

Q21A. For the last complete fiscal year, how much money came from the following?
Income-regular offerings

	AOG	SBC	CATH	LUTH	PRES
<50,000	22	26	12	32	24
50,001 - 100,000	39	35	16	29	28
100,001 - 200,000	24	24	16	27	29
200,001 - 500,000	11	10	42	10	13
>500,000	4	6	14	1	6

Q21B. Income — special offerings

	AOG	SBC	CATH	LUTH	PRES
0 - 2,000	42	18	10	34	21
2,001 - 5,000	13	14	17	18	20
5,001 - 10,000	10	16	25	14	19
10,001 - 25,000	20	26	49	14	18
>25,000	16	26	51	21	22

Q21C. Income — special fundraisers

	AOG	SBC	CATH	LUTH	PRES
0 - 100	61	82	35	56	62
101 - 500	8	2	2	7	11
501 - 1,000	8	5	4	6	6
1,001 - 2,500	7	4	8	17	5
2,501 - 5,000	7	4	5	9	7
5,001 - 10,000	6	1	8	3	6
>10,000	4	2	38	4	3

Q21D. Income — wills, bequests, and special gifts

	AOG	SBC	CATH	LUTH	PRES
0 - 100	80	77	39	46	54
101 - 500	8	2	6	7	7
501 - 1,000	1	3	4	3	2
1,001 - 2,500	3	1	9	11	8
2,501 - 5,000	3	5	6	9	7
5,001 - 10,000	3	4	30	14	16

Q21E. Income — investments

	AOG	SBC	CATH	LUTH	PRES
0 - 100	84	74	36	40	24
101 - 500	5	8	4	14	12
501 - 1,000	3	5	8	7	8
1,001 - 2,500	3	4	16	13	20
2,501 - 5,000	1	4	8	9	11
5,001 - 10,000	3	1	10	8	12
>10,000	1	5	18	10	15

Q21F. Income — rents and fees

	AOG	SBC	CATH	LUTH	PRES
0 - 100	80	84	49	53	46
101 - 500	1	4	5	5	10
501 - 1,000	1	1	4	8	4
1,001 - 2,500	1	1	10	9	7
2,501 - 5,000	6	7	13	11	13
5,001 - 10,000	5	1	8	7	10
>10,000	7	3	10	7	11

Q21G. Income — judicatory subsidies

	AOG	SBC	CATH	LUTH	PRES
0 - 100	97	97	86	92	88
101 - 500	1	1	0	0	3
501 - 1,000	0	0	2	2	0
1,001 - 2,500	0	0	3	1	1
2,501 - 5,000	1	0	3	0	1
>10,000	1	2	4	2	4

Q21H. Income — other

	AOG	SBC	CATH	LUTH	PRES
0 - 100	87	94	60	77	76
101 - 500	2	1	1	5	0
501 - 1,000	1	2	1	2	1
1,001 - 2,500	2	2	5	7	6
5,001 - 10,000	1	1	10	2	3
>10,000	6	1	14	3	7

Q21I. Total income

	AOG	SBC	CATH	LUTH	PRES
<50,000	18	22	8	20	14
50,001 - 100,000	31	31	11	28	23
100,001 - 200,000	30	24	17	32	31
200,001 - 500,000	17	14	36	17	23
>500,000	4	9	29	3	9

Q22. Capital campaign last year?

	AOG	SBC	CATH	LUTH	PRES
Yes	25	26	22	29	36
No	75	74	78	71	64

Q23A. Congregation have endowment?

	AOG	SBC	CATH	LUTH	PRES
No	97	84	17	42	44
Yes	3	16	83	58	56

Q23B. Amount of endowment

	AOG	SBC	CATH	LUTH	PRES
<50,000	97	91	57	61	64
50,001 - 100,000	2	6	11	21	5
100,001 - 250,000	2	4	17	15	16
250,001 - 500,000	0	0	12	0	8
>500,000	0	0	3	4	8

Q23C. Use of endowment income

	AOG	SBC	CATH	LUTH	PRES
General operating budget	1	4	3	18	23
Capital improvement	1	8	3	20	20
Special programs	0	5	3	21	21
Other	0	7	8	14	9

Q24A. Congregation expenses — operations

	AOG	SBC	CATH	LUTH	PRES
<50,000	24	30	8	24	15
50,001 - 100,000	33	29	17	30	27
100,001 - 200,000	26	20	21	29	30
200,001 - 500,000	12	15	39	15	21
>500,000	4	6	14	3	7

Q24B. Expenses — school subsidies

	AOG	SBC	CATH	LUTH	PRES
0 - 100	91	99	31	94	90
101 - 500	1	0	1	0	1
501 - 1,000	1	0	0	1	2
1,001 - 2,500	1	1	4	0	1
2,501 - 5,000	1	0	0	1	2
5,001 - 10,000	2	0	7	4	1
>10,000	4	1	55	0	1

Q24C. Expenses — denominational program

	AOG	SBC	CATH	LUTH	PRES
0 - 100	3	0	1	2	1
101 - 500	4	2	0	0	1
501 - 1,000	4	2	1	5	3
1,001 - 2,500	15	6	4	8	9
2,501 - 5,000	17	11	7	13	12
5,001 - 10,000	23	19	18	20	28
>10,000	34	60	69	51	46

Q24D. Expenses — other

	AOG	SBC	CATH	LUTH	PRES
0 - 100	56	50	64	24	14
101 - 500	7	6	3	13	11
501 - 1,000	5	9	2	11	10
1,001 - 2,500	10	11	8	22	10
2,501 - 5,000	10	12	6	12	18
5,001 - 10,000	4	8	6	11	14
>10,000	7	5	12	8	23

Q24E. Total expenses

	AOG	SBC	CATH	LUTH	PRES
<50000	18	23	7	18	12
50,001 - 100,000	31	30	12	28	25
100,001 - 200,000	28	24	16	33	32
200,001 - 500,000	19	15	34	17	23
>500,000	4	9	31	4	9

Q25A. Congregation have mortgage?

	AOG	SBC	CATH	LUTH	PRES
Yes	62	47	32	37	23
No	38	54	68	63	77

Q25B. Annual mortgage payment

	AOG	SBC	CATH	LUTH	PRES
<2,000	18	51	23	14	44
2,001 - 5,000	13	4	2	5	9
5,001 - 10,000	13	7	10	16	11
10,001 - 25,000	21	23	11	32	7
>25,000	35	15	55	34	30

Q26. Who was involved in the preparation of the budget?

	AOG	SBC	CATH	LUTH	PRES
Pastor	77	82	94	82	82
Paid staff	20	39	52	18	24
Governing board	80	41	34	89	91
Finance committee	31	94	83	64	87
Cong members	10	46	8	26	28

Q27. Who has *final* say in approving the budget?

	AOG	SBC	CATH	LUTH	PRES
Pastor	16	0	69	0	0
Governing board	43	0	8	0	91
Finance committee	0	0	11	0	1
Cong members	25	98	0	100	6
Pastor & governing board	11	0	0	0	0
Pastor & finance comm	0	0	2	0	0
Pastor, board & finance board	2	0	6	0	0
Board & finance comm.	0	0	2	0	0
Other	3	2	1	0	2

Q28. What strategies were used to encourage lay-giving to support the congregation's operating budget last year?

Q28A. Sermons on stewardship

	AOG	SBC	CATH	LUTH	PRES
Pastor only	70	64	41	67	69
Laypersons only	0	0	5	0	0
Pastor and laypersons	20	24	28	24	24
No sermons	10	12	26	9	7

Q28B. Appeals or testimonials during worship

	AOG	SBC	CATH	LUTH	PRES
Pastor only	15	10	30	4	5
Laypersons only	9	15	8	33	38
Pastor and laypersons	20	24	28	24	24
No appeals	14	23	30	29	13

Q28C. Distribute promotional material

	AOG	SBC	CATH	LUTH	PRES
At church only	22	33	19	4	9
Mailed to members only	3	2	8	7	9
At church and mailed	34	42	48	81	75
No promo material	41	23	26	8	7

Q28D. Phone every member

	AOG	SBC	CATH	LUTH	PRES
Pastor only	0	0	0	0	0
Laypersons only	1	1	3	4	8
Pastor and laypersons	7	2	0	1	1
Not phone	92	97	97	95	92

Q28E. Visit every member

	AOG	SBC	CATH	LUTH	PRES
Pastor only	4	0	0	0	0
Laypersons only	0	2	0	11	17
Pastor & laypersons	7	2	1	7	3
Not visit	89	96	99	82	80

Q28F. Phone some members

	AOG	SBC	CATH	LUTH	PRES
Pastor only	6	0	3	0	0
Laypersons only	0	2	10	16	30
Pastor and laypersons	7	5	5	3	5
Not do partial phone	87	93	82	81	65

Q28G. Visit some members

	AOG	SBC	CATH	LUTH	PRES
Pastors only	8	1	4	0	0
Laypersons only	1	3	3	15	22
Pastors and laypersons	6	8	9	7	8
Not visit	86	88	85	78	70

Q29. In your program to encourage giving, which had the greater emphasis?

	AOG	SBC	CATH	LUTH	PRES
Percent of income	66	45	19	40	23
Support programs	11	20	47	30	41
Half and half	15	25	19	24	29
No program	8	10	16	6	8

Q30. Did your congregation use any of the following?

	AOG	SBC	CATH	LUTH	PRES
Pledge cards	43	18	46	59	89
Numbered envelopes	19	65	94	93	87
Monthly/quarterly receipts	23	39	16	72	68
Annual receipts	77	61	50	67	68
Other	6	9	6	9	6

Q31. What procedures were used concerning mailing in contributions?

	AOG	SBC	CATH	LUTH	PRES
Postal envelope provided	1	2	8	10	17
Postal envelope not provided	86	90	81	90	83
Mailing discouraged	14	8	11	1	1

Q32. What is your congregation's emphasis with regard to the biblical standard of tithing?

	AOG	SBC	CATH	LUTH	PRES
Tithe due God	99	81	5	2	14
Tithe not obligatory	2	9	17	34	32
Proportion of income emphasized	0	7	58	58	42
Proportionate giving not emphasized	0	3	20	6	12

Q33. Which of the following is emphasized most strongly in your congregation?

	AOG	SBC	CATH	LUTH	PRES
Commit lives to Christ	50	54	5	10	21
Change society structures	0	1	3	2	8
Follow teachings of Jesus	50	45	62	63	67
Part in church tradition	0	0	30	25	3

Q34. What is your congregation's approach to interpreting and teaching the biblical meaning of Christian faith and the Church?

	AOG	SBC	CATH	LUTH	PRES
Our church true interpretation	79	65	83	24	7
One true interpretation	12	24	1	25	27
Many valid interpretations	9	11	16	51	66

Q35. Does your congregation teach that Christian life should be safeguarded through abstinence from:

	AOG	SBC	CATH	LUTH	PRES
Food	7	5	13	0	0
Alcohol/tobacco	94	85	4	4	5
Gambling	90	81	2	2	6
Movies/dancing	90	59	10	1	2
Other	25	31	37	8	18
None stressed	4	9	45	86	79

Q36. In general, how would you describe your congregation's teaching in relation to "typical" churches in your denomination?

	AOG	SBC	CATH	LUTH	PRES
Allow more differences	12	18	13	14	20
Similar to typical	79	75	80	83	58
Stricter	9	8	7	4	23

Q37. Last year what emphasis did you give to the biblical concept of stewardship of God's gifts?

	AOG	SBC	CATH	LUTH	PRES
Year 'round	55	36	16	27	23
Occasional	45	58	44	64	66
Once	0	4	19	5	10
No emphasis	1	2	21	4	2

Q38. How was stewardship emphasized?

	AOG	SBC	CATH	LUTH	PRES
Sermons	96	94	70	91	92
Lay testimonials	66	59	28	51	65
Religious education	75	72	9	55	44
Church newsletter	51	56	65	89	87
Other	15	13	21	30	32

Appendix B

Responses to
Lay Questionnaires

This appendix gives percentage responses to all items on the lay questionnaires. The number of cases were: Assemblies of God, 1,915; Southern Baptists, 1,883; Catholics, 2,194; Evangelical Lutheran Church of America, 2,470; and Presbyterians, 2,440. All the data were weighted to represent a random sample of laypersons in each denomination. Columns may not total to 100 because of rounding.

Q1. How long have you been attending worship services in your congregation?

	AOG	SBC	CATH	LUTH	PRES
Less than one year	6	3	2	2	1
1-2 years	15	9	6	7	7
3-5 years	23	15	13	13	13
6-10 years	24	14	15	13	16
11-20 years	19	19	20	19	22
Over 20 years	13	41	45	47	42

Q2. Does your congregation have serious financial needs?

	AOG	SBC	CATH	LUTH	PRES
Yes, very serious	11	6	6	9	8
Yes, somewhat serious	29	31	33	38	32
No, only routine	42	50	38	40	45
No, financially well off	6	6	6	4	5
I don't know	12	6	18	10	9

Q3. Do you feel you have enough information about the handling and allocation of funds by the leaders of your congregation?

	AOG	SBC	CATH	LUTH	PRES
Yes	71	81	53	73	76
No	20	12	28	16	15
No opinion	9	8	19	10	9

Q4. Do you feel that typical members of your congregation have enough influence in decisions about the use of church money?

	AOG	SBC	CATH	LUTH	PRES
Yes	67	79	48	69	70
No	19	15	25	20	19
No opinion	14	7	27	11	11

Q5. How much do you trust the handling and allocation of funds by the leaders of your congregation?

	AOG	SBC	CATH	LUTH	PRES
High	81	81	66	69	73
Medium	17	18	31	28	26
Low	2	2	3	2	2

Q6. How much enthusiasm do you feel, in general, about the work and programs of your congregation?

	AOG	SBC	CATH	LUTH	PRES
Very high	33	26	17	16	22
Moderately high	49	52	51	55	56
Moderately low	12	16	18	19	16
Very low	3	3	6	5	4
Generally opposed	0	0	0	0	0
No opinion	3	3	8	6	3

Q7. In the last year did you, or another adult in your family, fill out a pledge card or commitment card regarding church giving for the year?

	AOG	SBC	CATH	LUTH	PRES
Yes	31	29	52	60	79
No	67	69	45	39	20
Don't know	2	2	3	2	1

Q8. Do you approve or disapprove of the practice of asking lay members of the congregation to fill out annual pledge cards or commitment cards regarding church giving for the year?

	AOG	SBC	CATH	LUTH	PRES
Approve	37	41	48	58	78
Disapprove	46	47	38	32	15
Don't know	17	12	14	10	7

Q9. Do you prefer that clergy (priests or ministers) or lay leaders handle financial matters in your congregation?

	AOG	SBC	CATH	LUTH	PRES
Clergy	3	1	10	1	1
Combination	82	65	78	68	68
Lay leaders	9	28	4	23	27
No preference	7	6	9	8	5

Q10. Has your congregation actively promoted a "stewardship approach" to the giving of time, talent, and money which teaches the spiritual meaning of how we use God's gifts?

	AOG	SBC	CATH	LUTH	PRES
Yes-give more	42	34	20	28	35
Yes-no effect	30	38	44	53	51
Yes-give less	0	0	1	1	1
No	15	17	10	8	6
Don't know	13	11	25	10	7

Q11. How do you make decisions about how much money to contribute to your congregation?

	AOG	SBC	CATH	LUTH	PRES
Tithe	73	44	4	7	9
Annual percent	3	7	6	8	9
Annual amount	2	9	14	22	41
Weekly amount	8	19	39	38	25
Can afford each week	15	22	37	26	15

Q12. Do you feel that lay members have sufficient influence on the decision-making in your denomination?

	AOG	SBC	CATH	LUTH	PRES
Yes	66	68	49	66	69
No	20	22	27	16	19
No opinion	14	10	24	18	12

Q13. Does your denomination as a whole (nationwide or worldwide) have serious financial needs?

	AOG	SBC	CATH	LUTH	PRES
Yes, very serious	4	9	13	7	10
Yes, somewhat	18	33	38	35	34
No, only routine	38	31	23	23	22
No, financially well off	3	2	7	2	2
Don't know	38	25	20	33	32

Q14. Do you feel you have enough information about the handling and allocation of funds by the leaders of your denomination?

	AOG	SBC	CATH	LUTH	PRES
Yes	54	51	34	46	46
No	27	33	46	33	36
No opinion	19	16	20	21	18

Q15. How much do you trust the handling and allocation of funds by the leaders of your denomination?

	AOG	SBC	CATH	LUTH	PRES
High	68	43	46	47	43
Medium	29	45	45	48	44
Low	2	13	9	6	13

Q16. For supporting mission projects of your denomination, either overseas or in this country, do you prefer that the denomination select and fund the mission projects or do you prefer that you select the mission projects to which to give?

	AOG	SBC	CATH	LUTH	PRES
Denomination	19	35	23	23	20
Self	25	16	31	20	25
Combination	51	43	36	46	49
No opinion	5	6	10	11	6

Q17. Do you read any magazines, newspapers, or newsletters published by your denomination or a denomination-related group (e.g., diocese, synod, association, or convention)?

	AOG	SBC	CATH	LUTH	PRES
Regularly	40	45	36	34	24
Occasionally	40	34	36	38	38
Rarely	11	12	17	18	20
No	9	9	11	10	17

Q18. How much enthusiasm do you feel, in general, about the work and programs of your denomination?

	AOG	SBC	CATH	LUTH	PRES
Very high	34	18	14	10	10
Moderately high	47	51	50	47	47
Moderately low	10	18	19	23	24
Very low	2	5	6	6	8
Generally opposed	0	1	0	1	1
No opinion	6	8	10	15	10

Q19. Would you prefer that congregations make more decisions about funding programs, such as missions, outreach, and social service, rather than having denominational leaders decide?

	AOG	SBC	CATH	LUTH	PRES
More local decision making	36	50	44	50	56
Like situation now	48	37	33	29	29
More denominational decision-making	3	4	4	3	3
No opinion	13	10	20	18	12

Q20. Only followers of Jesus Christ can be saved.

	AOG	SBC	CATH	LUTH	PRES
Strongly agree	83	77	21	34	33
Moderately agree	3	7	14	18	16
Neither	3	6	17	20	20
Moderately disagree	1	3	15	12	12
Strongly disagree	10	8	34	17	19

Q21. If I had to change the congregation I attend, I would feel a great sense of loss.

	AOG	SBC	CATH	LUTH	PRES
Strongly agree	51	51	39	36	39
Moderately agree	28	29	25	31	32
Neither	13	12	19	18	15
Moderately disagree	5	6	9	10	8
Strongly disagree	4	3	7	5	5

Q22. Opportunities to serve in lay leadership in my congregation are available if one is willing to make the commitment.

	AOG	SBC	CATH	LUTH	PRES
Strongly agree	73	79	63	68	70
Moderately agree	16	11	22	20	21
Neither	7	7	10	9	6
Moderately disagree	3	2	3	2	2
Strongly disagree	2	1	2	1	2

Q23. Important decisions about the life of my congregation are made with open discussion by church leaders and members.

	AOG	SBC	CATH	LUTH	PRES
Strongly agree	47	64	20	44	38
Moderately agree	25	23	27	33	35
Neither	13	7	31	12	13
Moderately disagree	8	4	12	7	8
Strongly disagree	7	3	10	4	6

Q24. The budget priorities of my congregation are appropriate.

	AOG	SBC	CATH	LUTH	PRES
Strongly agree	47	45	21	27	31
Moderately agree	27	35	32	42	41
Neither	19	11	37	18	17
Moderately disagree	5	6	7	8	8
Strongly disagree	3	3	3	4	3

Q25.My whole approach to life is based on my religion.

	AOG	SBC	CATH	LUTH	PRES
Strongly agree	75	59	40	31	31
Moderately agree	16	28	33	42	42
Neither	4	9	15	18	17
Moderately disagree	2	2	8	7	8
Strongly disagree	3	2	2	3	3

Q26.What religion offers me most is comfort in times of trouble and sorrow.

	AOG	SBC	CATH	LUTH	PRES
Strongly agree	33	34	38	30	22
Moderately agree	25	28	28	31	32
Neither	17	15	16	18	19
Moderately disagree	11	12	11	13	17
Strongly disagree	14	12	8	7	11

Q27.The leaders of my congregation are sufficiently accountable to members regarding how church contributions are used.

	AOG	SBC	CATH	LUTH	PRES
Strongly agree	58	63	30	45	46
Moderately agree	22	24	31	36	36
Neither	12	8	28	14	12
Moderately disagree	5	3	7	4	5
Strongly disagree	3	2	5	2	2

Q28.The leaders of my denomination are sufficiently accountable to members regarding how church contributions are used.

	AOG	SBC	CATH	LUTH	PRES
Strongly agree	39	27	18	21	18
Moderately agree	23	29	26	29	26
Neither	31	28	34	39	36
Moderately disagree	5	10	12	8	11
Strongly disagree	3	7	9	4	10

Q29. Overall, the pastor of my congregation is doing a good job.

	AOG	SBC	CATH	LUTH	PRES
Strongly agree	77	70	62	62	66
Moderately agree	16	19	25	24	22
Neither	3	5	7	7	7
Moderately disagree	3	3	4	4	3
Strongly disagree	2	3	2	3	3

Q30. Overall, the leadership of my denomination is doing a good job.

	AOG	SBC	CATH	LUTH	PRES
Strongly agree	56	29	34	28	22
Moderately agree	26	31	37	38	32
Neither	5	19	18	28	32
Moderately disagree	2	11	7	4	9
Strongly disagree	2	10	5	2	6

Q31. Overall, I approve of the decision-making process in my congregation.

	AOG	SBC	CATH	LUTH	PRES
Strongly agree	60	59	32	40	45
Moderately agree	24	29	40	41	40
Neither	8	6	19	11	8
Moderately disagree	6	5	6	6	5
Strongly disagree	2	2	3	2	2

Q32. Overall, I approve of the decision-making process in my denomination.

	AOG	SBC	CATH	LUTH	PRES
Strongly agree	43	23	21	19	17
Moderately agree	27	29	33	35	32
Neither	8	6	19	11	8
Moderately disagree	6	5	6	6	5
Strongly disagree	2	2	3	2	2

Q33. What do you believe the *primary* duty of Christians is?

	AOG	SBC	CATH	LUTH	PRES
Help others commit to Christ	60	56	6	14	16
Change unjust social structure	0	1	6	4	6
Follow teachings of Jesus	38	41	60	63	66
Participate in traditions and sacraments	0	1	22	11	5
Don't know	2	2	6	7	7

Q34. How often do you attend worship services at your church?

	AOG	SBC	CATH	LUTH	PRES
Never	0	1	1	1	1
Few times/year	1	3	6	8	8
Once/month	1	1	4	9	7
2-3 times/month	5	8	11	27	25
once/week	27	36	59	51	53
>once/week	66	51	20	4	7

Q35. How many hours, if any, during the last month have you attended programs or events at your church other than worship services?

	AOG	SBC	CATH	LUTH	PRES
0	14	9	51	37	32
1-2	11	8	23	22	18
3-5	28	27	14	24	24
6-10	24	32	8	12	17
11-20	13	16	3	4	6
>20	10	8	1	2	2

Q36. How many hours, if any, during the last month have you given volunteer time at your church to teach, lead, serve on a committee, or help with some program, event, or task?

	AOG	SBC	CATH	LUTH	PRES
0	31	25	63	45	41
1-2	16	17	13	19	20
3-5	21	24	12	19	19
6-10	18	19	6	12	13
11-20	8	10	4	3	5
>20	7	6	2	2	3

During the last year, approximately how much money did your household contribute to each of the following? Write your best estimate in the boxes provided and fill in the corresponding circles underneath. Use only whole dollar amounts; do not use "cents."

Q37. To your church, in regular giving (not including school tuition or contributions to a capital campaign). Include the value of material goods as well as monetary gifts.

	AOG	SBC	CATH	LUTH	PRES
0	1	2	2	2	2
1-100	3	4	9	9	6
101-250	4	4	12	10	8
251-500	8	9	25	18	17
501-1,000	12	14	32	22	22
1,001-2,500	31	31	15	28	29
2,501-5,000	28	25	3	9	13
5,001-10,000	11	10	1	2	3
>10,000	2	1	0	0	1

Q38. To your church, in giving to a special capital campaign for a new building or a new program.

	AOG	SBC	CATH	LUTH	PRES
0	50	50	47	54	50
1-100	19	17	26	20	15
101-250	9	9	13	8	10
251-500	12	12	7	8	11
501-1,000	6	6	4	6	7
1,001-2,500	3	4	2	3	5
2,501-5,000	1	1	0	1	1
5,001-10,000	0	1	0	1	1
>10,000	0	0	0	0	1

Q39. During the last year, approximately how much money did your household contribute to groups or causes in your denomination other than those described in questions 37 and 38?

	AOG	SBC	CATH	LUTH	PRES
0	18	21	18	28	26
1-50	24	30	34	35	31
51-100	19	19	19	17	17
101-500	26	23	21	15	20
501-1,000	7	5	5	2	3
1,001-2,000	3	2	2	1	1
>2,000	2	2	2	1	1

Q40. During the last year, approximately how much money did your household contribute to all religious groups or causes outside your denomination?

	AOG	SBC	CATH	LUTH	PRES
0	27	36	33	35	30
1-50	27	29	34	33	26
51-100	13	11	14	12	13
101-500	19	15	15	14	17
501-1,000	6	5	3	4	6
1,001-2,000	4	3	2	2	4
>2,000	4	2	1	1	4

Q41. During the last year, approximately how much money did your household contribute to non-religious charities, community organizations or social causes?

	AOG	SBC	CATH	LUTH	PRES
0	20	10	9	5	5
1-50	40	32	29	29	22
51-100	17	21	22	23	18
101-500	19	26	29	30	35
501-1,000	3	8	7	8	11
1,001-2,000	1	2	2	3	5
>2, 000	1	1	2	2	5

Are there situations under which you might consider donating more money to your congregation? I would give more money to my congregation if:

Q42. It were more spiritually nourishing

	AOG	SBC	CATH	LUTH	PRES
Yes	12	13	16	13	14
No	70	63	54	58	62
Don't know	18	24	30	29	24

Q43. The preaching were more meaningful

	AOG	SBC	CATH	LUTH	PRES
Yes	8	8	16	11	11
No	78	73	60	66	69
Don't know	14	19	24	24	20

Q44. It paid more attention to social issues

	AOG	SBC	CATH	LUTH	PRES
Yes	5	8	16	10	11
No	83	76	57	68	71
Don't know	12	17	27	22	18

Q45. It paid less attention to social issues

	AOG	SBC	CATH	LUTH	PRES
Yes	2	3	5	4	6
No	87	81	70	75	75
Don't know	10	15	21	20	16

Q46. The worship services were more traditional

	AOG	SBC	CATH	LUTH	PRES
Yes	4	5	12	7	7
No	87	80	67	73	77
Don't know	10	15	21	20	16

Q47. The worship services were more modern

	AOG	SBC	CATH	LUTH	PRES
Yes	2	2	8	5	4
No	88	84	72	75	80
Don't know	9	14	20	20	17

Q48. What is your sex?

	AOG	SBC	CATH	LUTH	PRES
Female	56	59	62	63	62
Male	44	41	38	37	38

Q49. What is your age?

	AOG	SBC	CATH	LUTH	PRES
<18					
18-25	0	0	0	0	0
26-30	3	2	1	1	1
31-35	7	4	4	4	3
36-40	14	11	12	10	9
41-45	15	11	10	10	12
46-50	11	9	10	10	8
51-55	8	8	8	10	8
56-60	8	9	8	8	7
61-65	7	10	10	10	10
66-75	10	18	18	17	20
>75	4	9	10	11	14

Q50. How would you describe yourself?

	AOG	SBC	CATH	LUTH	PRES
Asian/Pacific Islander	1	0	5	0	0
African-American	2	1	1	0	2
Hispanic	5	0	5	0	0
White	91	96	88	99	97
Naive-American	1	1	0	0	0
Biracial	1	1	1	0	0

Q51. Which of the following best applies to you currently?

	AOG	SBC	CATH	LUTH	PRES
Single	6	4	8	5	6
Committed relationship	1	1	1	1	1
Married	79	78	71	78	74
Separated	2	0	1	1	0
Divorced	6	5	6	5	5
Widowed	7	13	13	11	14

Q52. If you are currently married or living in a committed relationship, does your partner attend the same congregation you do?

	AOG	SBC	CATH	LUTH	PRES
Yes	72	73	64	72	67
No	9	8	12	9	11
Does not apply	18	19	25	19	23

Q53. What is your highest level of education?

	AOG	SBC	CATH	LUTH	PRES
High school or less	34	29	28	28	16
Some college	41	39	32	35	31
College grad	17	20	20	22	30
Graduate degree	8	12	20	15	23

Q54. About how much income did your family or household receive last year from all sources before taxes?

	AOG	SBC	CATH	LUTH	PRES
<10,000	8	6	8	6	4
10,000-14,999	9	8	9	9	6
15,000-19,999	9	7	7	8	7
20,000-29,999	18	17	17	16	13
30,000-39,999	18	16	14	17	16
40,000-49,999	13	14	13	14	12
50,000-59,999	10	14	10	10	13
60,000-69,999	6	7	7	7	8
70,000-79,999	4	6	4	5	6
80,000-99,999	3	4	5	5	7
100,000-149,999	1	2	4	3	6
>=150,000	1	1	3	2	4

Q55. How many dependent children (under 18 years of age) do you have living with you?

	AOG	SBC	CATH	LUTH	PRES
0	52	65	60	65	68
1	15	11	13	10	11
2	19	17	16	16	16
3	9	6	7	7	5
>=4	4	2	5	2	1

Q56. How many dependent children (under 18 years of age) in your household attend religiously affiliated grammar school or high school (Catholic, Lutheran, etc.) five days a week?

	AOG	SBC	CATH	LUTH	PRES
0	89	96	87	97	97
1	7	2	7	2	2
2	4	1	3	1	1
3	1	1	1	1	1
>=4	1	0	1	0	0

Index

About the Author

Charles E. Zech is a professor of economics at Villanova University. His graduate work was done at Notre Dame. He has worked on a wide variety of research projects. His previous books include *Plain Talk About Churches and Money* (with Dean Hoge and Patrick McNamara), and *Money Matters: Personal Giving in American Churches* (with Dean Hoge, Patrick McNamara, and Michael Donahue). He is the author of dozens of articles and has spoken to many parish groups on the topic of giving.